BikerCraft

This book wouldn't have happened without the help and support of my long-suffering better-half Kaz, who came-up with the idea of the book in the first place. My grateful thanks also go to my very close friend Professor Jatin for really putting this book through it's paces and Jester, who's input has been invaluable since I began this project. I would also like to thank my close friend Lez, for his priceless help with this during the past 5 years. Cheers !

Contents

This manual gives you a phenomenal amount of information, in a format which I hope you'll find easy to wrap your head round and fully understand. Contained within these pages is a wealth of knowledge which, one day, may save your life or the life of someone else. With constant practice, your riding abilities and confidence will improve but you must remember that 'Rome wasn't built in a day' and that it will take time for you to master all of these skills. But, if you apply what you learn in this book, you'll be surprised how quickly it becomes second-nature ...

Disclaimer :- Within this manual are instructions that need to be carried-out which, if done incorrectly, could result in serious injury or even death. Any manoeuvre should only be done **If It Is Safe To Do So**. Rather than repeat that instruction throughout the rest of this book, I'm going to abbreviate it now to :- **IIISTDS (If It Is Safe To Do So)**(pronounced eye-stids) and this subject is covered in more detail in Chapter 2.

Obviously, you should never attempt any manoeuvre whereby doing so would put your life, or the life of somebody else, in danger. And finally, I would like to make it clear that neither the author, nor anybody else however involved in the production or distribution of this manual, accept any liability whatsoever for any injuries or damages, however caused, whilst learning any of the techniques described herein. In other words, however it went wrong, it wasn't my fault.

Also, there are frequent quotes and references, throughout this book, to the Highway Code. To most people, the Highway Code is just something that they have to learn for their test and then they will forget most of it. Ignorance, especially in the eyes of the Law, is no excuse but knowledge can sometimes give you the upper hand. With that in mind, I've included a few motorcycle-specific rules, together with some Statutory Laws, which you may find useful one day.

Chapter One - BikerCraft's System of safe motorcycle control

Introduction

It's only when you've first got your full motorcycle licence that people will say to you "now that you've passed your test, you'll have to learn how to ride properly." There's more truth to that statement than most people realise, but where does a newly-qualified rider learn from ? There are plenty of books, videos and courses to help you pass your test but after that, it's purely down to you to improve your riding skills, usually by trial and error. Unfortunately, a very high proportion of newly-qualified riders will crash due to inexperience, overconfidence, or a mixture of both.

Passing your bike test should be considered as being only the start of your learning how to ride competently and you should always be looking to improve your riding standard because where riding a motorcycle is concerned, you should never stop learning.

Riding a motorbike, regardless of your own ability or experience, immediately makes you more vulnerable to the careless actions of others or mistakes made by yourself. Not every accident can be put down to 'human error' though because sometimes they just happen completely out of the blue with no fore-warning. However, around 95% of all crashes are caused by human error by the rider, by another road-user, or a mixture of both. But don't be put off by this fact, because the aim of this book is to help keep you out of the '95% club' by teaching you BikerCraft's System together with hints, tips and proven advanced riding techniques.

Introduction to BikerCraft's System

The Home Office commissioned the first edition of 'Roadcraft' in 1973 which described the Police's 'System.' Roadcraft still remains as the Standard by which the most professional and respected riders in the world, the police, ride to. Although the concepts of Roadcraft were adopted by both RoSPA (Royal Society for the Prevention of Accidents) and the I.A.M. (Institute of Advanced Motorists) as the de facto guide to riding at an Advanced level, there was a flaw. Without the benefits of hi-vis bike, siren, blues and Legal Authority, the raising of the risk factor when riding like a Police Officer is continually ignored. Indeed the advice given in Roadcraft is deemed, by a number of respected barristers, as downright dangerous as it continually focuses on 'making progress' (hard acceleration) and riding at what are considered 'extremes' without the benefits of risk mitigation. Riding an everyday bike on everyday roads requires a totally different approach and attitude, which is where BikerCraft comes in.

The aim of this book is to try and convey the advanced riding techniques described in the 'Roadcraft' manual in a way which is easier to understand for the everyday rider, whilst retaining the proven concepts of 'The System' of safe road-riding. At first, some of the steps may seem a little complicated but with continual practice and application of BikerCraft's System, they will become second-nature to you. Just like most other things in life 'practice makes perfect' and you'll probably surprise yourself at just how quickly you'll pick it up. Whether you're a novice rider, a rider returning to motorcycling or a rider looking to enhance your existing skills, this book aims to teach you the techniques which may, one day, save your life or the life of somebody else. BikerCraft's System is fully compatible with, or exceeds, the DVSA's motorcycle test Standard so you could even use this book to help you pass your test (if you haven't already done so).

As an analogy, let's suppose you want to learn to play a musical instrument, which you don't know how to play. The sales person in the shop shows you a few basic chords which you feel confident that you could easily learn, so you buy the instrument and take it home. It would only be a matter of time before you would realise that you will need more tuition, especially as the sales-person made the basic chords look so easy to do. It's only by dedicated learning, and an enormous amount of constant practice, that you would start to become skillful. Exactly the same rule applies to motorbikes. Just because you may have passed you DVSA test does not, by any means qualify you as an accomplished rider.

Nor could you consider yourself a competent rider if you haven't ridden a bike for the past 10, 15 or 20 years, no matter how good you might think you once were. This book hopes to give you the extended knowledge in order for you to be a safer and more confident rider out on the road. The System of riding has a proven track-record of eliminating or reducing potential and real hazards. Just like learning to play a musical instrument, it might seem impossible at first, but with practice and experience comes mastery. Every musician has had to learn the basic 7 notes, at some point in their lives, and BikerCraft's 'System' consists of just 6 basic steps. That's the initial, basic introduction over with, so let's start at the beginning :-

BikerCraft's System

By having a universally methodical, practical approach to riding means that you will, with plenty of practice, learn how to perfect those techniques and eventually master the art of motorcycling, on any given road, in whatever circumstances. As you learn how to be a better rider, the increased knowledge and experience that you gain will give you capability and confidence. Build your knowledge up gradually and remember that you must never, no matter how confident that you feel, ride above your limits, or outside the limits of the road, or your bike. A simple formula to help you to remember that is :- High self-belief x limited skill = high crash / injury probability. Long before the credit card for the repair bill hits your doormat, your pride and your confidence will have taken a thorough beating. Getting carried-away on the road could lead to you getting carried-away on a stretcher or in a body-bag. Overconfidence is something that you will have to watch out for but if you stick within the guidelines of BikerCraft, and self-analyse your own riding as you go along, you should be fine. One thing that you should constantly be doing whilst riding a motorcycle is assessing hazards, but what exactly is a hazard ? The answer is simple :-

Anything that is, or could potentially be, a danger to you.
In terms of riding a motorcycle, that encompasses just about everything around you but a hazard can be broken-down further into three different types :-

Physical features – the actual road itself including junctions, roundabouts, hills, dips, bollards, bends and turns.

Other road users – cyclists, pedestrians and vehicles whose positions, actions or movements could create a hazard.

Environment - variations in road surface (pot-holes, gravel, painted lines) or climate conditions (such as rain, ice and high winds).

But there is another hazard that will always be present whenever you're out riding, and that's the nut holding the handlebars ! Your own state of mind can severely affect the amount of concentration that you should be dedicating to the road / traffic conditions. If you're worried, anxious or fretful about something then you will not be able to give the road your full attention and you might not notice the hazard until it's too late. Or if you're over-excited and giddy, your decisions won't be fully thought through properly and you won't assess hazards as you might normally do. If you're not concentrating fully, then you're just an accident looking for somewhere to happen.

A hazard situation starts before you even set-off riding because, at some point, you will have to join other traffic using the road. As soon as your bike is moving, everything around you, especially ahead of you, poses a potential risk. When you are walking along an empty pavement, you only need to look just ahead of your feet in order to avoid any obstacles but when you're riding a motorbike, things change dramatically due to the fact that you could be travelling 10 times faster than a pedestrian can walk. On a motorcycle, you need to be effectively scanning the road ahead, to the rear and to the sides of you, in the near to far-distance, to give you a better awareness of your surroundings. If you only look 20ft straight ahead of you when you're riding, you're going to end-up with a season ticket to your local A&E Department, or have undertakers gleefully rubbing their hands together expectantly every time you take your bike out. BikerCraft deals with this too.

At 30 MPH, how far do you think that you would travel in just one second ? The answer, which may surprise you, is 44 ft (13.41 m). At an average walking speed of 3 MPH it would take about 20 minutes to walk one mile but at 30 MPH it would only take 2 minutes. The person walking would have only covered 176 (out of 5,280) feet in that time (53.64 metres out of 1609.34 metres). The formula is constant, so at 60 MPH you would travel 88 feet (26.82 metres) in just one second, and takes only 1 minute to travel 1 mile. The person walking would have only covered 264 feet (80.46 metres) in that time. Or, put another way :

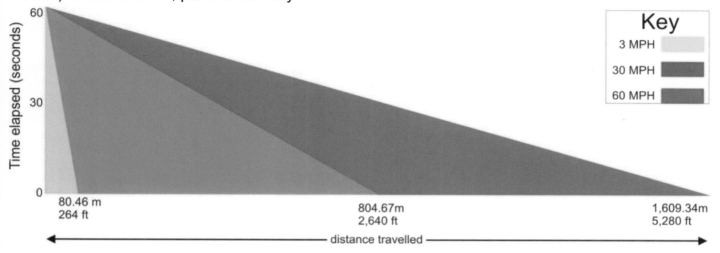

So let's imagine the scenario :- It's a busy Saturday afternoon as you ride down a typical high street at 30 MPH. There are parked cars on both sides of the road and a steady flow of slow-moving traffic in both directions. There is a passenger-laden bus stopped on the right-hand side in a lay-by. The pavements are bristling with shoppers of all ages. Close your eyes and picture the image in your mind for a minute and then count how many potential hazards that you see. Then you see a warning sign on your left for a staggered junction 100 metres ahead. Don't forget to account for the time elapsed, and the distance you would have travelled since this exercise began. If it takes you 2 or 3 seconds to imagine the scenario, readjust your mental image to take into account that you will have travelled between 88 ft (26.82 m) and 132 ft (40.23 m) in that time.In the following example, the black and white blocks denote 44 ft (13.41 m) which would be the distance travelled in1 second. A standard UK double-decker bus is about 49 ft (14.93 m) long and Is represented by the red rectangles. The yellow dots represent lamp-posts at about 120 ft (36.5 m) apart to give you some idea of scale :-

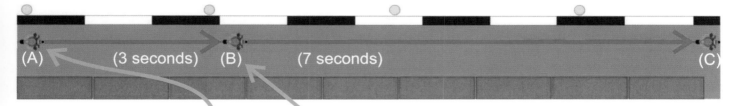

If the exercise started here, you'd be here in just 3 seconds having travelled 132 ft (40.23m) - nearly 3 double-decker buses !

In this example, it would only take 10 seconds to travel 440 ft (134.11 m), the equivalent of nearly 9 double-decker buses. Your brain will need to be taking-in a lot more information, and processing that information, a lot quicker than normal. The rider at points (A) and (B) should already be looking well ahead, where the rider a point (C) is shown, in order to identify any potential hazards and plan accordingly for them well in advance. Observation and Concentration go hand-in-hand.

Now close your eyes and count again. Let's add a couple of erratic cyclists and some pot holes, randomly scattered into the scenario, then we'll add those to your running total. Now we'll throw in some dark thunder clouds, pouring rain and bright headlights reflecting off the glossy road surface into the equation. Count again. I'm not trying to put you off, it's just that I'm trying to get across how much concentration is needed, at all times, when riding a motorbike. But don't worry, because BikerCraft will give you the skills you need to help you deal with every type of situation.

Let's now take it to the other extreme. Imagine you're on a remote, isolated, perfectly straight, well-maintained road on a sunny day with nothing else around for miles. How many hazards do you see now ? But life isn't like that for most of us so there has to be a universal, structured, methodical approach as to how hazards are recognised and assessed before any action is taken, by you, to deal with them.

If we use this diagram as a very basic guide and assume that at point (A) you are travelling at 30 MPH and that by point (C) you need to be doing somewhere between 5 and 10 MPH in order to make the left turn safely.

As well as slowing down, you should also give other road users ample warning as to your intentions using the bike's indicators, and make sure that it is safe for you to complete the entire manoeuvre. At its most fundamental level, you will have to indicate, slow down and then turn, but none of those processes allow for ensuring your safety, which is why you need to learn, and implement, BikerCraft as part of your everyday riding. Also, for the purposes of this example, every hazard has been removed, which is not really indicative of riding on today's busy roads.

Whilst 'The System', as described in the Police's Roadcraft manual, works for riders of bikes equipped with high-visibility day-glo rectangles, blaring sirens, two-tone horns and the word 'POLICE' splattered across the fairing screens (and the ability to unnerve anybody that they choose to follow), it doesn't work so well in the real world for the rest of us. Even if you went to the extent of bedecking yourself from head to foot in Day-glo and painting your bike to look just like a copper's bike, it certainly doesn't guarantee that you'll be seen. It may, however, see you on a charge of 'impersonating a Police Officer', which is a very serious offence! ('Polite' riders beware.) No matter what you wear, no matter how bright your headlight is or what colour-scheme your bike has, never assume that any of that will make a blind bit of difference to any other road-user who's not paying proper attention in the first place.

Everyday riding, on everyday roads, for everyday people requires, as I've said before, a different technique and that technique is called BikerCraft . With ever-increasing traffic congesting the roads on a daily basis, there are more and more hazards that you will have to contend with, requiring a higher level of observational skills by you so there needs to be a methodical structure that you can use which will make you a more competent and more skill-full. BikerCraft is all about being aware of what's going on around you and you won't be able to do that if you're not concentrating at all times. You need to be aware of what's going-on around you, especially ahead of you, and to the sides, and using that information, and the knowledge and experience that will gain from this book, to make a better judgement of what course of action you're going to take next. And the next Course after that, but you will only be able to do that if you are **Concentrating / Observing,** anticipating situations and applying BikerCraft's System to your everyday riding.

In it's simplest format, BikerCraft breaks down everyday manoeuvres and situations into parts which, like links in a chain, are merely components to be pieced together as necessary. Let's go back to the music analogy and remember that whatever song you have ever heard, consists of just 7 basic notes. But, before we get down to business and learn BikerCraft System's constituent parts, we need to start with **Concentration / Observation**. Whenever you are riding, this is the one thing that you should be doing **AT ALL TIMES** ! If you don't Concentrate, if you don't take effective Observations, you're gong to hurt yourself or somebody else, it's that simple. Think of it as '**Riding Rule #1**'.

Now let's look at the various steps which make-up BikerCraft's System :-

       (1)   **Course**

       (2)   **Rear observation / signal**

       (3)   **Speed / gear**

       (4)   **Forward hazard assessment**

       (5)   **Mirror check / speed check**

       (6)   **Lifesaver**

I'll explain each section in detail in the next few pages but, these are all of the components that you will need. Each step also matches the left / right turn and overtaking diagrams shown in Chapters 2 and 3, so it might be an idea for you to memorise each step before we go any further. BikerCraft's System is described over the next few pages, after which I'll show you a few diagrams of how each component is used to make entire manoeuvres. Don't worry, it's not rocket science In fact, most of it is just plain, old common sense and you'll probably surprise yourself how quickly it becomes second-nature to you, with constant practice.

(1) Course – The bike's direction of travel and your positioning of it on the road. Manoeuvres such as turning right or overtaking a parked vehicle would usually require the machine to be placed to the right hand side of the lane whilst turning left might require the machine to be more over to the left-hand side of the lane.

This example shows a rider on a left-hand course who could be preparing for a left-hand turn, or is potentially avoiding an on-coming vehicle which may be overtaking a parked car, or is approaching a right-hand bend or is giving way to an on-coming vehicle.

This example shows the rider on a right-hand course who could be preparing to turn right, is about to overtake a parked vehicle, is giving a hazard a wide berth or is about to enter a left-hand bend.

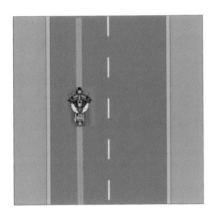

In the final example, the rider is close to the centre of the lane keeping an equal distance between the kerb and the centre white line which, generally speaking, should be the safest course but when you add-in all of the hazards on today's roads, everything must become more fluid and adaptable.

(2) Rear Observation / Indicator signal – Be aware of, and keep an eye on, the environment behind you by using both your mirrors and by taking frequent rear-observations over your shoulder. If you are going to alter your Course, plan it in plenty of time, and signal your intentions to other road users in advance of your planned manoeuvre. Before actually executing any manoeuvre, you will need to assess the traffic all around you to make sure that it will be safe for you carry it out. Depending on factors such as traffic conditions, road conditions, weather conditions etc. depends on whether it's better / less-harardous to use just your mirrors or turning your head to take a look over your right shoulder instead. Your mirrors have 'blind-spots' (explained on page 9) so get used to using your mirrors in conjunction with your RearObservations so that you will have a pretty fair idea of what's going- on all around you at all times. Sometimes, the Graphic may show just a Rear Observation, just anIndicator or both, as shown here :-

Rear Observation   Signalling (right)   Rear Observation / Signal

(3) Speed / Gear – The speed of the bike should always be matched by the engine speed using the appropriate gear because different gears work better at different road speeds. Your road speed is indicated by the bike's speedo and your engine speed is indicated by your rev-counter / tachometer. The bike must be immediately responsive to the throttle, as that can help with either braking or accelerating in the event of an immediate hazard.

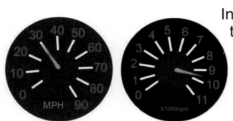

In the first example, the gear selected is too low, meaning that the bike is revving (screaming it's head off) at the upper end of the power range. The bike's engine probably wouldn't have a lot of acceleration left at this point but could potentially cause the bike to become unstable if the throttle was fully closed suddenly. Also, your fuel efficiency would be terrible !

Here, the bike is in too high a gear which would result in very slow If any) acceleration if the throttle was suddenly opened fully. The engine would struggle to produce any meaningful power, make a 'tinkling sound' and might evenstall. Large-capacity engines usually have a lot of torque ('pulling-power') but torque should never be confused foracceleration as they are two entirely separate things. Torque will eventually provide acceleration but is no substitute for being in the right gear at the right time. By the same rule, closing the throttle would result in the bike's engine not slowing the bike down very much, especially when compared to being in too low a gear or the correct gear.

This example shows that the revs are somewhere around the lower-middle third of the bike engine's range which should provide for a more responsive throttle whether it is suddenly opened or closed. Some motorcycle instructors call this a 'happy' engine.

During braking, as your road-speed decreases, remember to ensure that the road-speed matches the engine speed. Work down through the gears progressively, neatly and smoothly at the appropriate time, keeping the engine speed matched to your road speed. In the example shown here, even though the road-speed has *decreased* by 10 MPH, the engine's speed is still about the same as before. This process is repeated each time you change down a gear until you're in 1st gear, at which point you can decrease your speed down to a stop, if necessary.

Whilst accelerating, change to a higher gear at the upper end of your rev-range, preferably before the engine starts screaming it's nuts off, so that the bike's engine is still responsive to the throttle. Most rev-counters have a 'red-zone' which you should try and avoid going in to whenever possible.

The above examples are only meant as an introductory guide and you'll have to learn for yourself where your bike's engine speed needs to be for the engine to be 'happy'. High-revving 'race-replicas' will be totally different to, say, a large-cc Cruiser or a 4-stroke off-road bike and this is explained in Chapter 4.

Most riders don't even need to read the tacho / rev counter as they learn to listen to their bike's engine. They will know, just by listening, when it is in a responsive gear and will be used to the 'feel' of their bike's gears and engine. This will come to you with enough time and practice.

In it's simplest format, BikerCraft breaks down everyday manoeuvres and situations into parts which, like links in a chain, are merely components to be pieced together as necessary. Let's go back to the music analogy and remember that whatever song you have ever heard, consists of just 7 basic notes.

(4) Forward Hazard Assessment – Riding at 30 MPH, you'll cover a distance of 44 ft (13.41 m) per second so the environment around you can change constantly so you need to be ready for anything that might affect you. **Riding Rule #1.** You need to be pro-active as then deciding on the appropriate action to take. Here, we see that you were riding along your **Course (1)** when the car in front suddenly pulled up to the kerb but because you were paying attention and saw the hazard, you can immediately start to plan how you are going to deal with it.

The first question you must ask yourself is "why has the car pulled up ?" Is it because the driver is intending to park the car ? Is the driver merely pulling over to make a phone call ? Or is there something on-coming which has forced the driver to pull right over to the left of the lane ? Is it safe for you to overtake the vehicle ? Do you need to stop or slow down ? Only by paying **attention** and **concentrating** on what's going on around you, will you be able to make a proper decision as to what steps to take next.

In the diagram on the left, a **Forward Hazard Assessment (4)** lets you see theparked car, as well as the driver who has just got out of the car and is stood inthe road. In the diagram on the right,

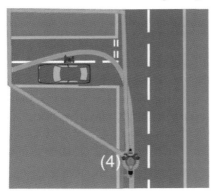

you are looking forwards in the opposite lane for any on-coming traffic, as well as looking into your intended junctionto assess any potential hazards BEFORE you commit to the turn.

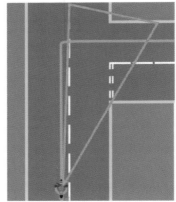

(6) Lifesaver

The last step before any turn or deviation is done involves a look over the relevant shoulder to check for anything in your mirrors and blind-spots. It is absolutely no use doing your Lifesaver whilst you're actually executing the manoeuvre as it will prove utterly worthless at that point. If through, your own laziness, you nonchalently do a Lifesaver as you turn, at least you'll know what

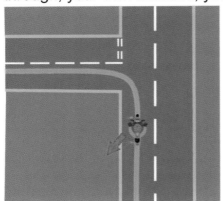

the vehicle looked like that you crashed into ! The Lifesaver is always the very last thing that you do before you actually manoeuvre your machine. If you're turning left or pulling your motorcycle over to the left, then you look over your left shoulder, if you're pulling out to your Right, then you look over your right shoulder, it's that simple. Honestly !

Most mirrors fitted to motorcycles are pretty useless, as about half (or more) of the visible range is usually obscured by your or your pillion's arms / shoulders (and the problem only gets worse with camping gear etc. loaded on) which doesn't leave much rear-ward visibility available to be used effectively. Most objects directly behind you, or to your rear-right or rear-left would be undetectable using just your mirrors, which is why you need to take effective Rear Observations in conjunction with your mirrors.

The areas marked in green show the limited view available using just the mirrors. Blind spots are shown in red.

This example clearly shows the extended range of visibility when a Lifesaver is done

(1) Course – Before completing a turn, you must select a safe course which will not immediately place yourself in a potentially dangerous or hazardous situation. Plan your route ahead in plenty of

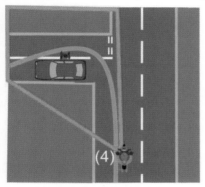

time, don't ever wait until during, or after you've executed your turn, to decide which Course you're going to use. In the first example, you are about to execute a left turn into the side-road and can see the parked car in the side-road. Immediately, you can plan to alter your course to take the parked car into account and simply take a wider line going in to the side-road (**iiistds**).

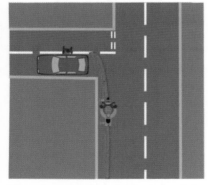

If you don't look ahead, and if you don't plan ahead, then you will, probably, end-up reacting at the last minute to the parked car. You will be forced to rush the overtaking manoeuvre through your own lack of forward-planning and that's just the type of situation which can, and generally does, lead to you having an accident.
Concentration / Observation !
Riding Rule #1

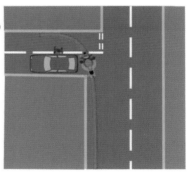

Never accelerate too fast for the conditions or where there is restricted forward visibility. If you are travelling behind another vehicle, be careful not to accelerate so much that you break the '2 second rule' (Highway Code Rule 126). (We'll go intto more detail about the 2-second rule in later chapters) Another consideration is to try and keep your bike on the correct side of the road, particularly when entering a left-hand bend, as using any on-coming traffic as an aid to braking tends to hurt ! Similarly, if you're entering a right-hand bend, running wide out into the kerbstones, hedges or garden walls tends to invalidate any possible future warranty claim. Conversely, accelerating too slowly could also put you at risk as vehicles could run into the back of you. Never execute a manoeuvre which causes another road user to have to change their Course, Speed or Direction. Also bear in mind that when you're riding a motorcycle these days, riding away from one lot of potential hazards merely puts you straight in amongst the next lot, most of the time, in most of the places that you will ride. No sooner have you completed one manoeuvre, you're on to the next.

(1) Course – With the exception of the pulling-up or parking manoeuvres and, arguably, crashing or falling off, before you even complete manoeuvre, another **Course (1)** has already started, so you continually need to read and assess the environment ahead, behind and around you. Remember, **Riding Rule #1 - Concentration / Observation**.

There's another component of BikerCraft's System which doesn't really have a specific place because it can be used at any time whatsoever, and that's the bike's horn. Your horn should be used whenever you need to warn a pedestrian or other road user of your presence. Let's have a quick look at some possible definitions :-

A Valium-using car driver on the school run - complete with screaming kids in the back.

The Daily Commuter, over-tired and late for work.

Newly-qualified drivers who might be very under-confident or very over-confident.

OAP's doing their weekly drive to the shops.

Cyclists using their 'selective version' of the Highway Code - The 'MyWay' Code.

Truck / HGV drivers keeping one eye on their tacho as they race back to the depot before they reach their daily Driving Times Limit.

Sales Reps late for an 'important' meeting with a client.

Any driver using a mobile phone - with or without Bluetooth, or one who is singing away to the in-car Ghetto-blaster or else fiddling-away with the car's in-built controls.

A night-shift worker looking forward to going to bed after a long, boring shift.

The Daily Commuter, over-stressed and fed-up, who just wants to get home.

Obviously, the list goes on and on, but these are just a few examples of what you need to be looking out for.

But there's another reason that you might need to use your horn, and that's the pre-occupied pedestrian ! In today's modern, inter-connected world, it's very rare to see a pedestrian who is not using their Smartphone in some way or other. They might be busy updating their Social Status and that type is known as a 'Textrian,' whereas the ear-phone wearing pedestrian - engrossed in their music - is now known as a 'Podestrian'.

In Stockholm, Sweden, the Authorities have even gone to the extremes of creating a new sign in order to warn Textrians / Podestrians to pay attention to the road when crossing. The only problem to that idea is that the Textrian / Podestrian could be so engrossed in their phone, that they would probably walk into the sign's post !

Maybe, in the UK, we need to change the Pedestrian Crossing sign in order to reflect Modern times, and my idea would look something like this :-

Never assume that pedestrians, Textrians or Podestrians will even bother looking to see if a road is clear before crossing it as they will be too engrossed in their Smartphone App, up-dating their social media status, searching for a particular music track or watching a funny cat video. No matter what, it'll be up to you to look-out for them ! (Sometimes though, it can be quite amusing to watch them leap out of their skin as the blast from your horn wrenches them back to reality !)

iiistds (eye-stids) As I said at the very beginning of this book, and before we start to get into the nitty-gritty, I need to make one thing absolutely clear to anybody following the advice given in this manual, which is that every manoeuvre described in this book should be carried-out ONLY **if it is safe to do so. iiistds** - eye-stids ! If you do find yourself in a situation where it is **not** safe for you to complete your intended manoeuvre, then simply cancel that manoeuvre or correct the situation as necessary.

Overtaking Parked Cars
In the following diagram, you are on a Course (1) and would see (4) the parked car obstructing your Course. Would you just stick the indicators on and pull out ? Of course not !

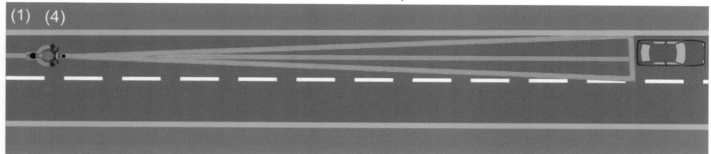

There is no provision for your safety if you chose to ride like that, and if we take a look, in the next diagram, at what's going-on behind you in the diagram above, we can see that a car is overtaking 2 other cars and would be on a collision course with you if you'd just stuck your indicators on and pulled out. It's also very doubtful that you would see the overtaking car in your mirrors either.

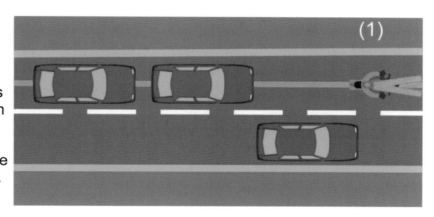

This is where BikerCraft's System comes in. If you refer back to BikerCraft System's Components diagrams earlier in this book, we can now look at making entire movements out of the separate actions, so let's bring some of them back and draw it out. This diagram shows the first steps which need to be carried-out at the beginning of an 'overtaking parked car' manoeuvre.

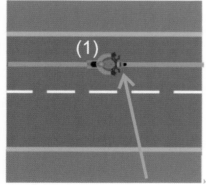

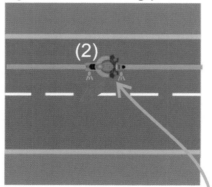

You're on your **Course, (1)** and see a parked car ahead (not shown in diagram).

The next step is for you to take a **Rear Observation (2)** your right shoulder and switch the right-turn indicators on.

After a few seconds with your indicators flashing, take another look, a **Lifesaver (6)**, over your right shoulder again to confirm whether the manoeuvre is safe to do (or not.)

If you continually practice, it'll soon become second-nature.

There will possibly be occasions where your **Course (1)**, for whatever reason, is closer to the centre white line when you need to turn left further up the road. In which case, simply have a quick glance **(2)** over your left shoulder, switch your left indicators on, leave it a few seconds and then do a **Lifesaver (6)** over your left shoulder before you move (**iiistds**)

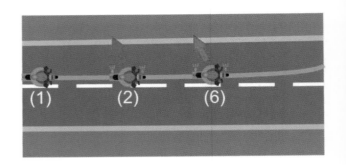

Now that you've got an idea about how the separate components can be used, lets now put a full manoeuvre together. This diagram shows the steps necessary to overtake a parked car with you, the rider, already on your **Course (1)** :-

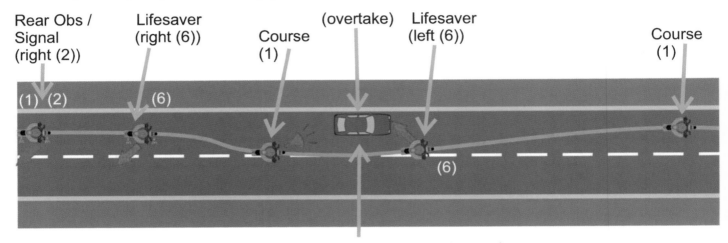

Leave at least a car door's width (**iiistds**)

As soon as you are on your (new) **Course (1)**, it becomes your **Course (1)** again and, as you can see, it's a never ending cycle until either you complete your journey and park your bike up, crash or fall off ! Because you are **Concentrating and Observing (Riding Rule #1)**, you will have already seen the parked car and will know that, at some point, you're going to have to pull out. You also know that you need to signal your intentions to other road users and give them ample warning of your intended change of **Course (1)**. Take a look over your right shoulder and assess any following traffic and as you do so, switch your right indicators on (**Rear Observation / Signal (2)**). By now, you shouldn't need to look where the switch is, it should be automatic but if it isn't, then I strongly suggest you practice it on a stationary bike until it is. After your indicators have been on for a few seconds, take another look over your right shoulder (**Lifesaver (6)**) to make certain that it is safe for you to pull more over to the right of the lane and get on to your new **Course (1)**. Remember to switch your indicators off. There might be a side-road up-ahead on the right, and you don't want to complicate things for yourself by confusing other road users. As you approach the parked car, look to see if there is any smoke coming out of the exhaust, (**Forward Hazard Assessment (4)**), try to see through, into the car, to see if anybody is sat in it. Assess any on-coimg traffic and look over the car to see if that gives you any better visibility. Be ready to sound your horn / swerve / brake.

The environment ahead of you will need to be scrutinised and assessed but that should have been taken care of by you already **Concentrating and Observing (Riding Rule #1).** Pass the parked car, leaving at least a door's width between you and the othervehicle (**iiistds**), and take another **Forward Hazard Assessment (4)**, which will dictate your next course of actions. Ask yourself, "are there any more parked vehicles to overtake?" "Are there any potential hazards ahead which would mean that the current **Course (1)** is the least hazardous ?""Is it safe to pull back in yet ?" "What's behind me ?"

We'll assume that the coast is clear and that your next plan is to pull over towards the middle of the lane but you can't assume that it is safe for you to do so, you have to check first by doing a (left) **Lifesaver (6)**. As one set of manoeuvres is complete, the next set has already started **(Course (1))**. **Concentration / Observation (Riding Rule #1).**

Obviously, the above illustration has been simplified to show the basics of BikerCraft's System in order that you might get the idea of what is involved. All hazards (potential or otherwise) have been removed but, as you can clearly see, it's not as complicated a manoeuvre as it might at first seem and with constant practice, it will quickly become second nature to you whenever you ride. Let's move on to something more realistic ...

The previous diagram is typical of instruction manuals, in as much as it doesn't really reflect today's, sometimes manic, modern-day riding conditions, so I thought I'd give you a more 'real-world' example which might look like this :-

It goes without saying that this situation is full of potential hazards and very real dangers. Any car door could open at any time, pedestrians could step into the road without warning or on-coming traffic could be forcing you to ride further over to your left than you would, perhaps prefer, sending you closer to the parked cars on the left-hand side of the road, reducing the amount of safe manoeuvrability available to you. This type of situation is becoming more and more common as the amount of traffic on today's roads increases and so, because of the increased risk, a more defensive riding style is required. You might legally be in the right, the other driver might be in the wrong, but it is you who will end-up in the local A & E department ! Where motorcycles are concerned, YOU are the 'crumple zone !' Did you spot the pedestrian in-between the cars ?

Left Turns

A left-turn manoeuvre is fairly straightforward so let's bring together some of the Base Components that you'll need to begin with.

By being alert and paying attention **(Riding Rule #1),** you will have seen the junction ahead (indicated by the orange triangle.) Before reaching there, you will need to have checked for any following traffic, indicated and slowed your bike down in order to take the turn at a safe speed.

You're on your **Course (1)** and see the junction up-ahead.

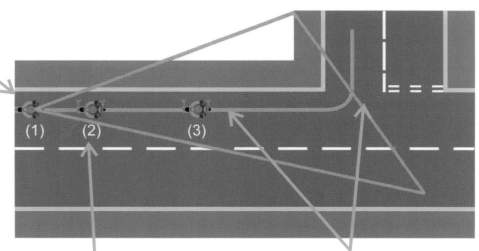

Take a quick glance over your **right shoulder (2)** to assess any following traffic and switch your left indicator on at the same time.

Keep an eye on the distance to the junction and reduce your speed gradually and change down the gears smoothly **(3)** as you approach the turning.

As you get nearer to the junction, keep looking to see into the road that you're going to be riding into. Look for stationary traffic which might be blocking the lane and look for pedestrians who might be about to cross the road or who already crossing the road.

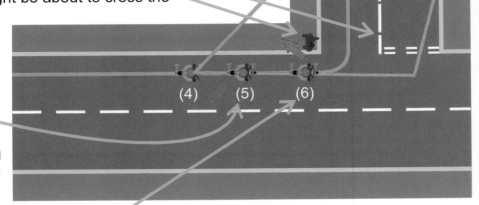

Do a quick mirror-check or take another glance over your right shoulder **(2)** to re-assess any following traffic, continue slowing down gradually until you're down into 1st gear.

Have a look over your left shoulder, **Lifesaver (6)**, <u>before</u> you get to the mouth of the junction, look again into the junction and plot your next **Course (1)**, based on what you see ahead of you. Don't do the **Lifesaver (6)** as you turn the corner as you need to be looking into the junction at that point.

We'll assume that there were no pedestrians, podestrians, textrians, other vehicles or road-users impeding your turn. (We'll get to that later). You should already be aware of what's ahead of you but always stay alert. Concentration / Observation - **RidingRule #1**.

As soon as you've completed the turn, switch your indicators off and choose your (new) **Course (1.)**

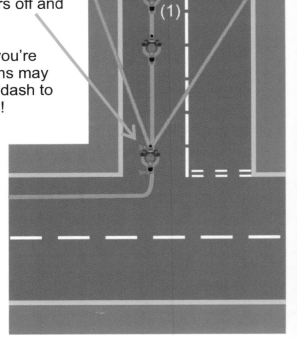

There may be parked cars on both sides of the street that you're riding into, cyclists weaving in and out or suicidal pedestrians may suddenly appear from between parked cars in a desperate dash to cross the road, sometimes pushing a pram in front of them !

As soon as the manoeuvre is complete, you're already on your next **Course (1)**

When you first start to incorporate BikerCraft's System into your own riding, you might find that you get your timings slightly wrong but with time and constant practice, all of these steps will become so natural that you won't even realise you're doing them every time. If you start them too late, just try to make sure that you don't end-up rushing the processes. Starting them too early might leave you feeling guilty about holding-up the traffic, or your intentions might be misunderstood by other road-users. Don't worry about it, learn from it and move on ...

If you were trying to memorise a new telephone number, for example, then you would probably break it down into smaller chunks and it will probably help if you do that with BikerCraft's System. Each component needs a certain amount of time and space to execute but some can be mixed together. Signalling / taking a Rear Observation can be combined, as can Mirror check / Speed with a Forward Hazard Assessment. The Lifesaver is <u>always</u> done on its own.

Instead of looking at the Left Turn in it's component parts,
lets put the whole thing together and see what it looks like :-

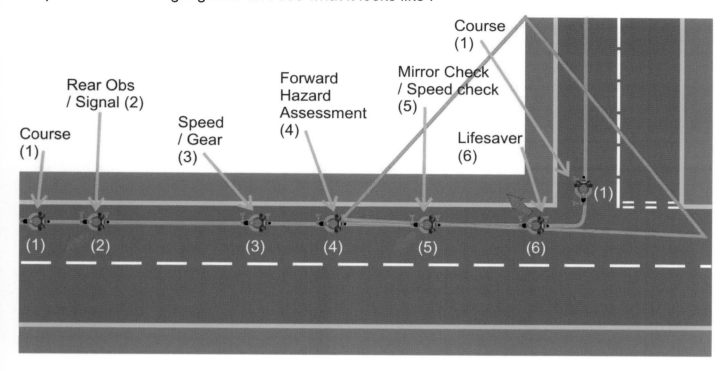

(If you need to, refer back to the previous break-down of the manoeuvre)

Just to re-cap, where **Speed / Gear (3)** is shown marks the point around which you will start to roll off the throttle and begin to decrease your speed gently. Ideally, your deceleration should be smooth and steady so that you are already in first gear by the time you reach point (6). Use **Forward Hazard Assessments (4)**, to assess what hazards might be lying in wait for you. Keep an eye on the following traffic by doing a quick **Mirror-check (5)** or by doing a quick shoulder-check. Sometimes, particularly in heavy traffic, it might be better for you to keep your eyes on the road immediately ahead of you. Make sure that you execute the **Lifesaver (6)** BEFORE you turn the handlebars. Take another look at your intended **Course (1)** to make certain that nothing has changed. Acceleration / deceleration will depend on the environment surrounding you, as well as ahead of you when you complete the turn.

As you carry-out this manoeuvre, you may at one time or another, encounter an impatient motorist who might try and force you and your bike into the gutter as you slow down to make the turn. The best way to deal with that kind of situation is to sound your horn and, defensibly, stand your ground. If you begin to feel intimidated by another road-user, hold a Course which is central to the lane because you have just as much right to use the road as anybody else. Always defend that right, but do it safely and always remember that a broken door mirror to a car could be a broken elbow to a rider. In some circumstances, it's better to yield a position than it is to force a bad situation into becoming worse. It's always the wiser person who knows when to give way, but don't ride submissively, ride correctly.

So, let's deal with **Normal Riding Position**, whilst we're on the subject. Realistically, there is no definitive 'normal riding position' as the real world is constantly variable and situations can change enormously. Never regard the gutter as part of the road - it's only a debris-laden drain. Remember that. A 'normal' riding position is always dictated by situations, circumstances and your environment. 'Normal' should be considered as any position which gives you the best visibility whilst offering the least hazardous route at any given moment, in any situation. As a default riding position, consider placing yourself just to the right of the lane's centre (**iiistds**).

BikerCraft's System applies to every type of left turns at junctions, irrespective of what type of junction it is. It makes no difference whether it's a side-road, a T-junction or a roundabout - they're all the same with the only difference being that at point (6) in the diagrams, there would be 'stop' or 'give way' signs as well as road markings across the road.

This illustration shows what I mean :-

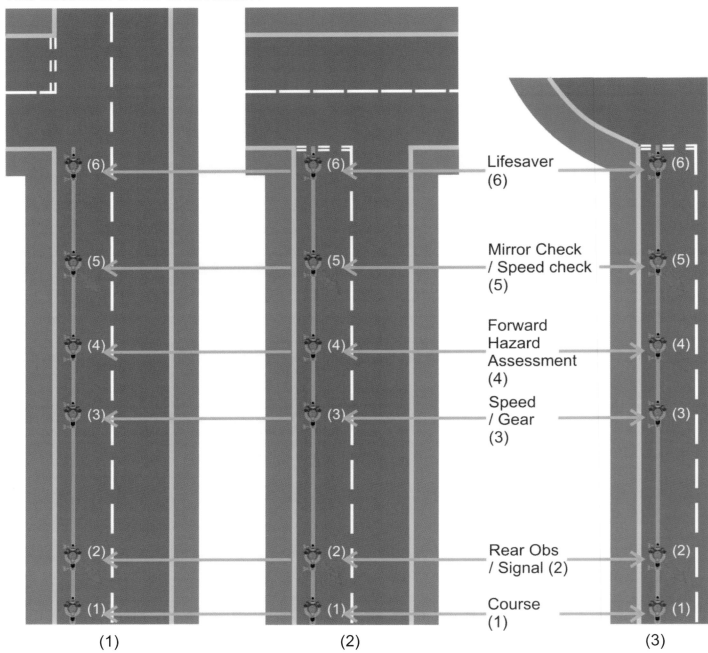

(1)   (2)   (3)

(Refer back to Chapter1 if you need to refresh your memory about any of the System's components.)

All 3 diagrams have been positioned so that the beginning of the side-road, the Give Way markings of the T-junction junction and the roundabout have all been aligned so that they are in exactly the same place in relation to each other. In all 3 scenarios though, as is clearly demonstrated, BikerCraft's System is exactly the same, irrespective of what type of junction it is. In diagram (1), you *should* have right of way but might need to give way to a pedestrian already crossing the road whereas in diagrams (2) and (3) you will have to be ready to give way, or even stop completely, depending on traffic, road markings and traffic signs. You should always complete any turn smoothly, neatly, with your machine under full control and having made sure that you don't cause anybody else to change their Course, Speed or Direction in doing so. The only difference between these turns is when executing a left turn at a roundabout, and we'll deal with that next.

When completing a left turn procedure at a roundabout, a LEFT **Lifesaver (6)** must be done before you begin to execute the turn onto the roundabout itself, and then you should keep approximately the same distance from the kerb as before you entered the roundabout.

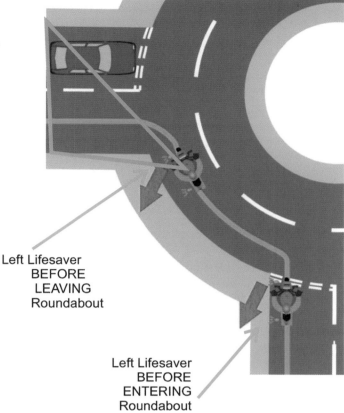

Look into the junction you plan to exit (if visibility allows) and plan your next **Course (1)** accordingly. The only exception to the normal rule is that when turning left exiting a roundabout, there is an extra LEFT **Lifesaver (6)**, which should be done just **before** you begin to exit the roundabout, and it's purpose is to make sure that nothing is trying to undertake you, which might catch you out.

Left Lifesaver
BEFORE
LEAVING
Roundabout

Left Lifesaver
BEFORE
ENTERING
Roundabout

Probably the most dangerous part of this entire manoeuvre is if you're entering the roundabout whilst following another vehicle. The vehicle in front of you might start to pull out, you would then automatically look right as you pull forward but whilst you're looking right, the vehicle in front might suddenly stop.

If you're lucky, if you're not accelerating too much, if the bike is upright and travelling in a straight line, on a good road surface and if there's enough room, you *might* be able to pull-up in time by doing an Emergency Stop. If not, you're probably going to end-up exchanging insurance details with the other driver whilst nursing a painful crotch area and looking over your bike to see what damage you've caused and how big the dent on your credit card's gonna be !

The simple solution is not to rush things, go with your own flow, and to give yourself a couple of seconds, after the other vehicle has begun it's manoeuvre, before you start your's.

Feeling confident so far ? We'll move on to the Right Turn / Overtaking manoeuvres, which look something like this :-

I've explained why the **Lifesaver (6)** is so important, but what action should you take if there is something actually approaching you up your inside that you've spotted ? Well, it all depends entirely on your environment, the roads around you, your course, your speed, your direction, your speed / gear, your intended manoeuvre, how quickly you spotted the hazard, the speed of the approaching hazard and how quickly you can react etc etc. Basically, I would suggest that your first option might be to try and resume your original course (**iiistds**) whilst sounding your horn and accelerating away from the hazard (**iiistds**). Another option, depending on all of the above-mentioned circumstances, might be for you to do an emergency stop (**iiistds**). If you're overtaking a moving car and it accelerates as you pass it (contrary to Highway Code rule 168), your choices are either to accelerate harder (if conditions, the speed limit etc allow and **iiistds**) or for you to slow down (**iiistds**).

Just to show how utterly important the **Lifesaver** can be, I thought I'd throw in a couple of examples of the types of roads which are becoming increasingly predominant in many towns and cities - bus lanes and cycle lanes.

Bus lanes, as you would expect, are a lot wider than cycle lanes and are generally found on major commuter routes in cities and towns. Buses (and in some areas taxis and solo motorcycles) are the only vehicles permitted to use them but there is an additional road user to be aware of, which is the cyclist. Bear that in mind when crossing a bus lane, particularly during rush-hour congestion. There may be stationary buses which allow you to turn left in front of them but you will need to ensure that your **Lifesaver (6)** takes into account cyclists, joggers etc who might be undertaking the bus.

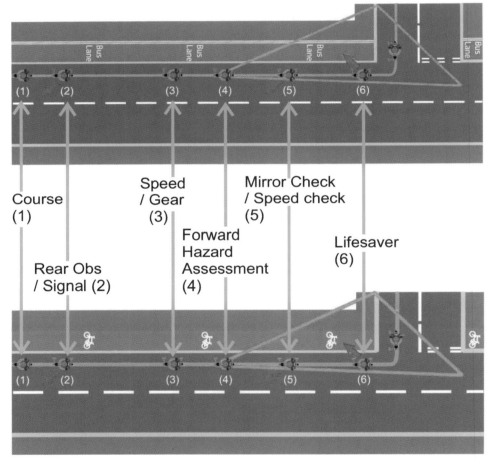

In this example, the **Lifesaver (6)** has to take-in the cycle lane, as well as the pavement, before the turn is executed as there may be cyclists or joggers, as well as pedestrians using the cycle lane, which could create a potential hazard at some point during the turn.

Again, if you need to, break the entire manoeuvre down as if you were remembering a new telephone number and practice the technique out on the road until it becomes second-nature.

Another real-world situation would be where there are multiple cars parked immediately just before a junction to the left.

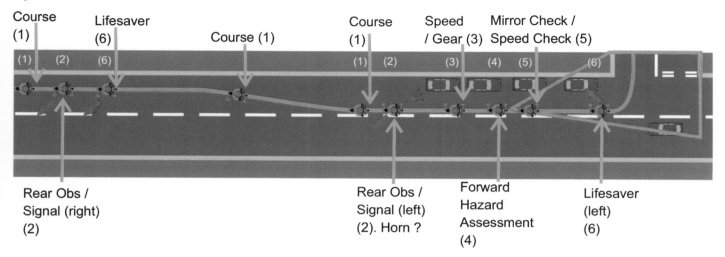

Course (1) | Lifesaver (6) | Course (1) | Course (1) | Speed / Gear (3) | Mirror Check / Speed Check (5)

Rear Obs / Signal (right) (2) | Rear Obs / Signal (left) (2). Horn ? | Forward Hazard Assessment (4) | Lifesaver (left) (6)

As you decide which **Course (1)** would be the *least* hazardous to travel, bearing in mind that there might be on-coming traffic, remember to cancel your indicators. Now you will have to concentrate on the much narrower field of vision immediately ahead of you and to each side (wherever you can). Re-assess any following traffic by taking either a look in your mirrors, or by doing a **Rear Observation (5)** over your right shoulder (depending on traffic conditions etc) and then turn your left indicators on. Doing it this way means that there is a small, but distinct, few seconds of time-lapse between left and right indicator signals which would signify - to a following vehicle that what you're now doing is a separate manoeuvre. As you approach the parked cars, - remember to look for fumes coming out of the exhaust (particularly in cold weather), remember to look through the cars, as well as over them, and sound your horn if it's use would be of benefit as a warning. Be aware that 'privacy glass' and panel vans will severely limit your range of visibility.

If, in the above example, a car door was to suddenly open right in front of you, then your only real options are to carry-out an Emergency Stop (**iiistds**) or swerve into the opposite lane (**iiistds**). This is the reason why you always need to remember **Riding Rule #1** - constant **Observation / Concentration.** The last **Lifesaver (6)** should also take into account not only the nearest parked car, but also any pedestrians or cyclists who's visibility to you may have been restricted by the parked vehicles (vans, mini-buses, trucks, buses, 4x4s etc).

You'll notice that even before one manoeuvre has finished, you've already started the next **Course (1).** All of the fresh hazards, potential or real, have to be fully assessed and it's a never-ending process of information gathering, assessing, concentrating, decision-making, planning, avoiding, defending whilst riding, that makes for a safer and more competent, confident rider. Only by keeping your wits about you, by **Concentrating and Observing (Riding Rule #1)** AT ALL TIMES, will you be able to make a proper, calculated decision in order to react to a potential or real hazard.

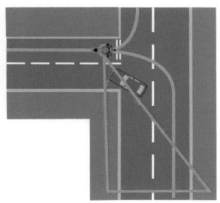

Another factor to consider is how to treat the signals of other road users and my advice would be "always with suspicion and caution !" In the first diagram, the rider is stopped at the give-way lines at the mouth of a T-junction and sees the vehicle approaching from the right which is indicating (it would seem) to turn left. It could be that the driver intends to pull-up just after the junction or maybe the driver hasn't made sure that the indicators are turned off from a previous manoeuvre. The best thing to do is wait until the other driver actually commits to the turn, as shown in the second diagram, before moving off (**iiistds**).

Chapter Three - Right turns / Overtaking

Right turns

As with the Left Turn Procedure in the previous Chapter, I've broken the Right Turn Procedure down into three bite-sized sections. These diagrams are not to scale, purely because that would take-up far too much of the page available.

Here, you're riding on your **Course (1)** at 30 MPH and see the right turn junction up-ahead.

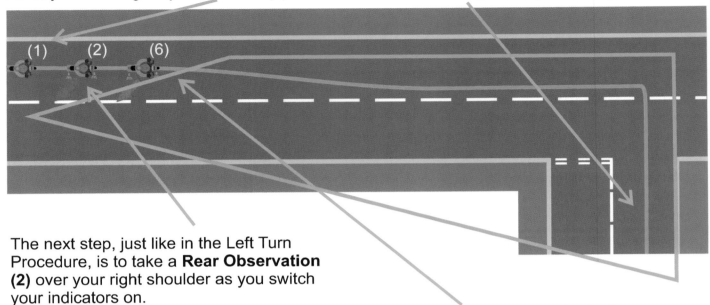

The next step, just like in the Left Turn Procedure, is to take a **Rear Observation (2)** over your right shoulder as you switch your indicators on.

After a few seconds of indicating right, look over your right shoulder, **Lifesaver (6)**, and plot your (new) **Course (1)** to be just left of the centre white line (**iiistds**) Take a **Forward Hazard Assessment (4)**

Obviously, you'll need to adjust your speed / gear during this process, which is something that you'll need to factor-in.

Move over towards the centre white line (**iiistds**) smoothly and neatly ...

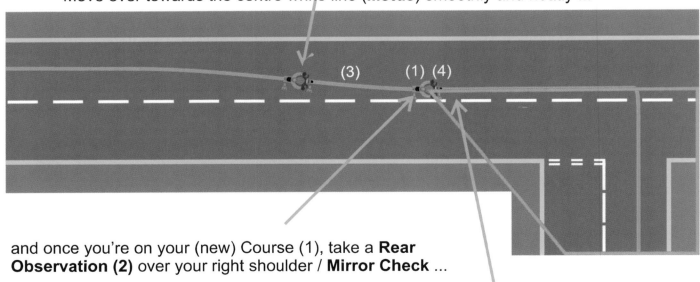

and once you're on your (new) Course (1), take a **Rear Observation (2)** over your right shoulder / **Mirror Check** ...

... before **Slowing Down and Changing Down (3)** through the gears. Keep an eye on the junction (**Forward Hazard Assessment (4)** and look for any changes which might force you to change your intended Course.

Whist still keeping an eye on the junction, slow-down and change down into 1st gear.

When the junction is clear, do a **Lifesaver (6)** over your right shoulder.

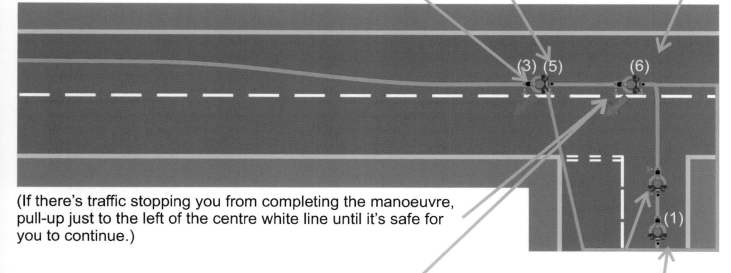

(If there's traffic stopping you from completing the manoeuvre, pull-up just to the left of the centre white line until it's safe for you to continue.)

Look forward again and then look into the turning before committing yourself to the manoeuvre **(iiistds)**. Look out for other road users who may stop in the junction, leaving you highly exposed in the middle of the opposite lane.

As soon as you're on your (new) **Course (1)** the manoeuvre is complete, and you're on **Course (1)**. Cancel the indicators and assess the hazards ahead. Acceleration, as in the Left Turns Procedure, should take into account any real or potential Hazards.

Just like the Left Turn Procedures, we'll now put the entire manoeuvre into one diagram, with all hazards (potential or otherwise) removed. You are travelling at 30 MPH and intend to turn right into the side-road that you've already seen. In comparison to the Left Turn Procedure, the only extra manoeuvres are a **Lifesaver (6)** over your right shoulder and the move out towards the centre of the road.

Course (1)   Lifesaver (6)   (new) Course (1)   Course (1) / Forward Hazard Assessment (4)   Speed / Gear (3) / Mirror check / Speed check (5)

Rear Obs / Signal (2)

Lifesaver (6)

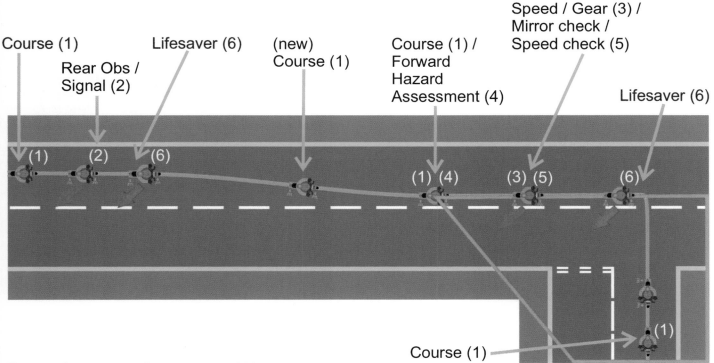

Course (1)

Remember, these diagrams are NOT to scale !

You should keep an eye on the junction as you approach it, so you will do more **Forward Hazard Assessments (4)** than are shown in the diagram, but you can easily fit it in after doing your **Mirror check / Speed check (5)** and checking your **Speed / Gear (3)**. Whilst doing your **Forward Hazard Assessment(s) (4)**, you might be able to look into the junction and so start to assess and plan the next stage of your manoeuvre. Watch to see if other vehicles are entering the junction and then braking suddenly as they enter the junction, as that would give you a good indication that there may be an unseen hazard waiting for you, literally, just around the corner. If another vehicle flashes it's headlights at you, it doesn't - necessarily - mean that it's safe for you to pull out. Always be wary and check - for yourself - that it's safe for you to carry-out your manoeuvre. If one road-user 'flashes' another road-user to pull out of a side-road / petrol station etc, expect the road-user who is pulling-out not to be looking properly - they will have assumed that it's safe for them to just pull-out.

In the example below left, you are shown to have limited visibility, and can only see the mouth of the junction but as you get nearer to the junction (shown in the example on the right) it is clear how much extra visibility is obtained when you can see right into the junction. It is at that point that the next **Course (1)** can be assessed, planned and plotted. Another example of why you need to always be **Concentrating and Observing (Riding Rule #1)**.

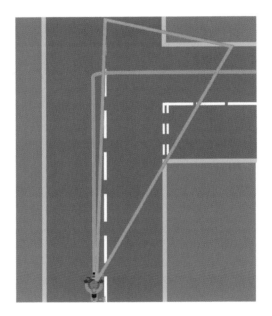
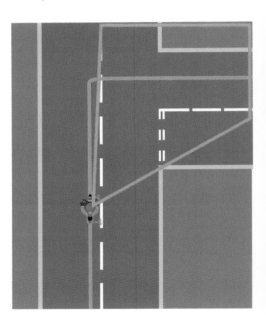

BEFORE the bike turns right, you must ALWAYS do a **Lifesaver (6)**. In the two examples shown below, the only difference is that I've added an impatient, inconsiderate driver into the equation. The car driver would be breaking the law and you would be in the right, but you would also probably end up in A&E (if you were lucky !)

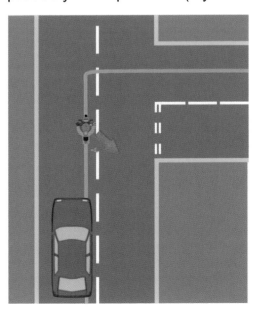

A simple **Lifesaver (6)** over your shoulder can help save your life. Hence the name !

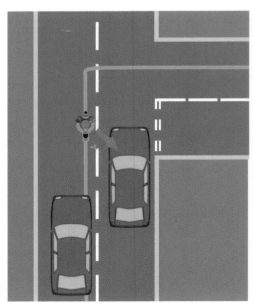

In this example of a 'T-junction', you'll notice that it is exactly the same System as you used in the right turn manoeuvre - there's absolutely no difference whatsoever. All-round visibility or traffic conditions may dictate that you might have to stop or give-way to traffic already travelling on the major road which would, usually, have priority. The junction may also be controlled by traffic lights or a stop sign, or might be an accident black-spot caused through a lack of visibility at the junction.

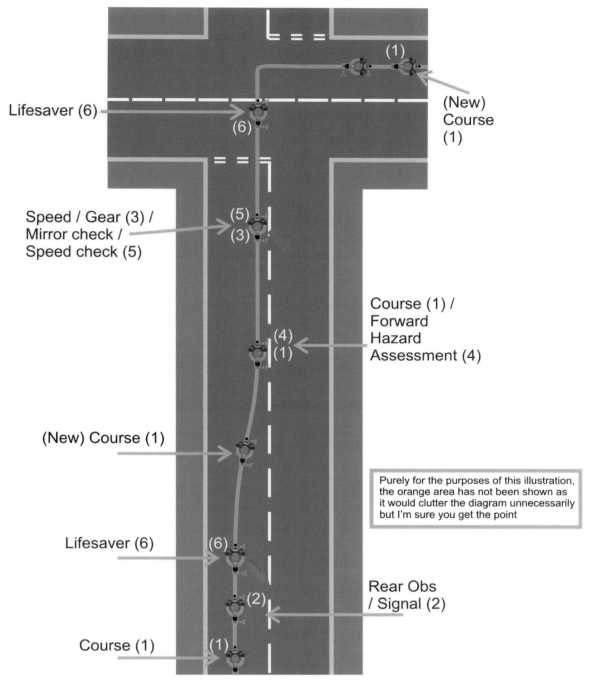

Lifesaver (6)

(New) Course (1)

Speed / Gear (3) / Mirror check / Speed check (5)

Course (1) / Forward Hazard Assessment (4)

(New) Course (1)

Purely for the purposes of this illustration, the orange area has not been shown as it would clutter the diagram unnecessarily but I'm sure you get the point

Lifesaver (6)

Rear Obs / Signal (2)

Course (1)

If there are no other road users whatsoever, you don't need to indicate. What's the point of indicating if nobody is going to see it ? Use your indicators only when you need to warn other road users of your intentions, that's what they're there for ...

Remember to cancel your indicators (if used) as soon as your turn is complete and you are on your pre-planned **Course (1)**. From the point where you are doing your **Forward Hazard Assessment (4)**, to where you are doing your last **Lifesaver (6)**, you need to be **Concentrating and Observing (Riding Rule #1)** everything in great detail ahead of you, to your forward-right and to your forward-left in readiness.

OK, here's a question for you - At what type of junction do you turn right by turning left twice ? Think about it for a while ...

Going back to my earlier question about what type of road junction means that you navigate it by turning left twice ...... The answer is, of course, a roundabout ! Below is a diagram proving that Statement :- (to reduce the amount of complexity, all Forward Hazard Assessments have been omitted from the drawing)

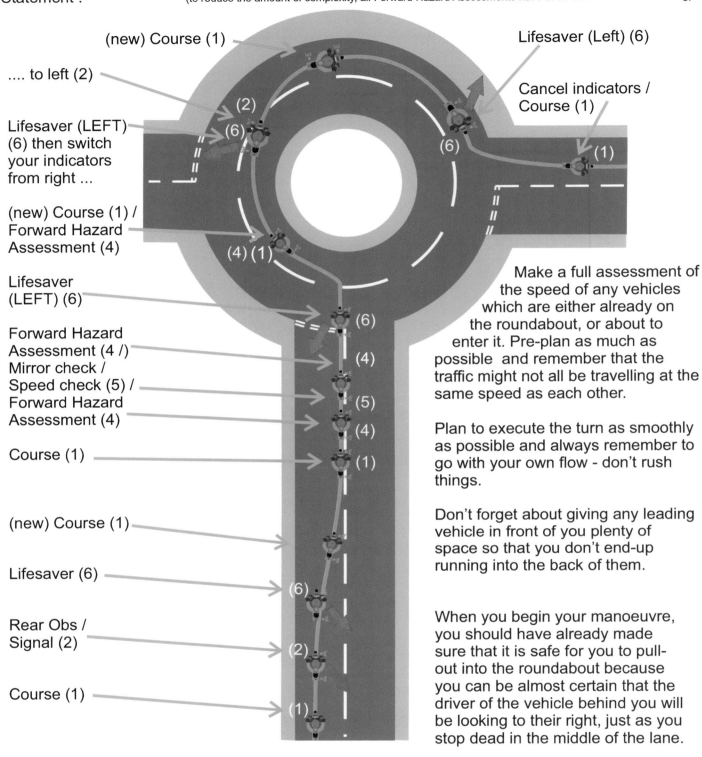

(new) Course (1)

.... to left (2)

Lifesaver (LEFT) (6) then switch your indicators from right ...

(new) Course (1) / Forward Hazard Assessment (4)

Lifesaver (LEFT) (6)

Forward Hazard Assessment (4 /) Mirror check / Speed check (5) / Forward Hazard Assessment (4)

Course (1)

(new) Course (1)

Lifesaver (6)

Rear Obs / Signal (2)

Course (1)

Lifesaver (Left) (6)

Cancel indicators / Course (1)

Make a full assessment of the speed of any vehicles which are either already on the roundabout, or about to enter it. Pre-plan as much as possible and remember that the traffic might not all be travelling at the same speed as each other.

Plan to execute the turn as smoothly as possible and always remember to go with your own flow - don't rush things.

Don't forget about giving any leading vehicle in front of you plenty of space so that you don't end-up running into the back of them.

When you begin your manoeuvre, you should have already made sure that it is safe for you to pull-out into the roundabout because you can be almost certain that the driver of the vehicle behind you will be looking to their right, just as you stop dead in the middle of the lane.

A right turn at a roundabout is probably the most challenging manoeuvre that there is because so much can happen in such a relatively small space. There's a massive amount of **Observation / Concentration (Riding Rule #1)** and **Forward Hazard Assessments (4)**, which all have to be done whilst keeping yourself safe. Due to the overall complexity of this manoeuvre, I've drawn an overview of all of the steps in this one diagram. I've broken certain sections of it down, in detail, in the diagrams in the following 2 pages.

The approach, as you can see from this diagram, is exactly the same as for the other types of right turn except one thing :- the **Lifesaver (6)** is ALWAYS over the LEFT shoulder when entering or leaving a roundabout. The reason for that is because as you enter or leave any roundabout, you *have* to turn left to do so.

Being totally honest with you, a right turn at a roundabout is probably the most complex and complicated manoeuvre possible, especially on multi-laned roundabouts with 5, 6 or more exits.

The example on the previous page is typical of an instruction manual so I thought I'd give you a better idea of what you might have to deal with in the real world. The green line shows your intended **Course (1)** but I've also overlaid it with the intended routes of just 6 (out of 17+) other road-users. Now you can see roundabouts can be quite tricky to negotiate !

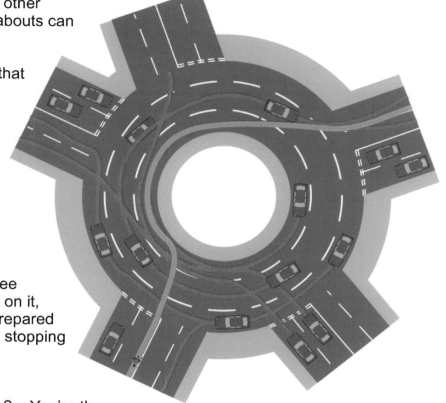

You can also see from this example that your **Course (1)** when navigating a roundabout is never a full circle, it's more of a spiral shape so maybe they should be called spiral-abouts rather than roundabouts ?

Whenever you're approaching a roundabout, early **Observations** are vital so that you get a better idea of what you're going to be dealing with. **Concentration and Observation (Riding Rule #1)** If you can clearly see that the roundabout hasn't any traffic on it, then you won't need to stop but be prepared for any vehicle directly in front of you stopping at the junction, and *then* looking.

Let's have another scenario shall we ?... You're the leading vehicle on the approach to a roundabout and you can see that there is a suitable gap in the traffic already on the roundabout. However, if you maintain your current speed, you will reach the junction of the roundabout before it is safe for you to pull out. You will have to pull-up but you already know that there is no traffic behind you. What do you do as you're approaching the roundabout ? The answer is to simply slow down sufficiently - in the correct gear - so that you time your entry onto the roundabout to coincide with the suitable gap. It's far safer, smoother and less stressful on you and your bike. Controlling your speed on the approach to the roundabout lets you enter it in a flowing manner, rather than in a rushed, panicking manner. Relax, and remember, go with your own flow. Riding smoothly will actually raise your average riding speed due to the fact that you will be stopping and starting less. If you have greater control of the situation and your bike, however big or busy the roundabout is, you won't get so stressed. Anticipate what other road users' actions might be and what direction they are meaning to head in, irrespective of which lane they're actually in. Just because another vehicle is in the lane to your left, doesn't mean that they don't intend to turn right ! Whenever you're on a large roundabout, keep an eye on the distances between you and the other vehicles to your left and right and be ready to sound your horn and take evasive action (**iiistds**)...

If you're negotiating a really large roundabout, doing left and right **Lifesavers (6)** from time to time will give you a better idea of what's going-on around you. Your mirrors are less than useless on a road where you're, possibly, at your most vulnerable !

As an example, one of the world's most notorious road junctions is the roundabout which encircles the Arc de Triomphe in Paris. One blog described this roundabout - "an accident happens there every 7 minutes and that there is not a single insurance company in the world that covers accidents within the roundabout. There are no lanes, and scores of cars race weave in and out of each other in packs. I like to call it "the traffic circle of death." After witnessing a van strike a motorcyclist and watching his bike slide across the pavement, I believe this." (source :- http://openroadtraveler.blogspot.co.uk/2010/07/paris-arc-de-triomphe.html)

The amount of observation required on the approach to a roundabout cannot be emphasised enough. Also, bear in mind that these diagrams are simplified and don't show any other traffic, other than you. Some roundabouts can be fast-moving at times, and totally clogged at others, so always keep your wits about you.

Pay particular attention where a roundabout is at the end of a dual-carriageway or motorway as the traffic exiting that type of road might be used to travelling at much higher speeds and so may make 'errors of judgement' when assessing other traffic (ie you !)

On your approach, take a look ahead / to your right **(4)** to assess If you will *have* to stop, the approach might not be clear, or the roundabout itself might be grid-locked. Look into the junction to see if there's any traffic approaching it which you might have to give way to.

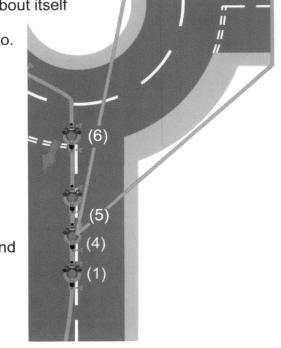

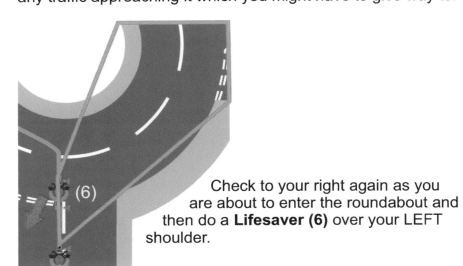

Check to your right again as you are about to enter the roundabout and then do a **Lifesaver (6)** over your LEFT shoulder.

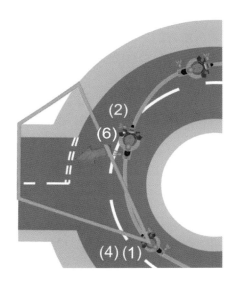

Watch for any traffic which may emerge from the turning on your left **(4)** and don't assume that, just because you have the right of way, some idiot won't try and cut you up. Just as you pass the last exit prior to the one that you want to take, switch your indicators from right to left and look ahead to start to plan your exit. Maintain a smooth, consistent **Course (1)** around the centre of the roundabout.

Your indicators will have informed other vehicles as to your intentions but you will need to make sure that it is safe for you to pull more over to the left-hand side of the lane by doing a LEFT **Lifesaver (6).** Make sure that your exit is clear **(4)**, then select your (new) **Course (1)**, **(iiistds)**, cancel your Indicators.

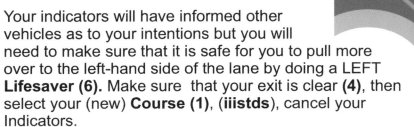

Overtaking

Whenever you approach a slower-moving vehicle, you will need to make one of two decisions, whether to overtake the vehicle or slow-down and match the other vehicle's speed. That decision will be based purely on road conditions, climate conditions, traffic conditions, the type of road, forward visibility, your machine's capabilities, your skill-level and the layout of the road itself. Is it sinking in yet ?

Before overtaking anything, you must fully assess the real and potential hazards and know what's going-on around you, it's not just a case of flicking the indicator switch on and cracking the throttle wide open because that sort of riding will, one day, get you killed. You will need to ask yourself a few questions like :- "are there any turnings coming up which the car might turn into?" "is there a junction, lay-by or petrol station up ahead - on the right - which might have traffic exiting?" (Bear in mind that the traffic exiting would only be looking to it's right, in the opposite direction to you.) "Is there any on-coming traffic?" "Are there any blind bends coming up?" "Will I be able to pass safely?" "Am I in the right gear?" "Is anything coming-up fast behind me?" "Am I already being overtaken myself?" "Is it necessary?" "Is it Legal?" (Highway Code #267) Never rush a decision and never get impatient but, rather, choose your time and place carefully, plan the manoeuvre and execute it smoothly and neatly. Job done !

Let's bring back the example of how to overtake a parked car, purely because it contains exactly the same steps as overtaking a moving car :-

Rear Obs / Signal (right (2))   Lifesaver (right (6))   (new) Course (1)   (overtake)   Lifesaver (left (6))   (new) Course (1)

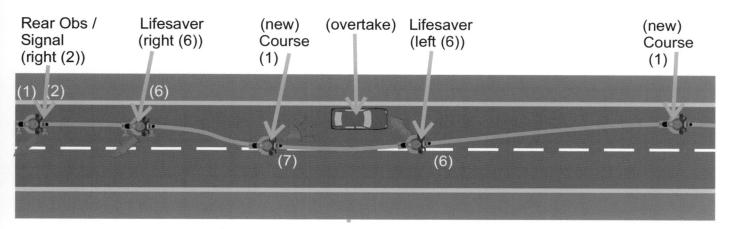

Leave at least a car door's width (**iiistds**)

The differences between overtaking a parked car and a moving car are the speed of the moving car and the car's position in the road. If you were riding along at 30 MPH and overtook the parked car, you and your bike would, obviously, be travelling 30 MPH faster than the stationery car but let's have the car travelling on a dual-carriageway at 30 MPH with you travelling 30 MPH faster than that, at 60 MPH :-

Course (1), Rear Observation / Signal (2   Lifesaver (6)   New Course (1)   Lifesaver (6)   (new) Course (1)

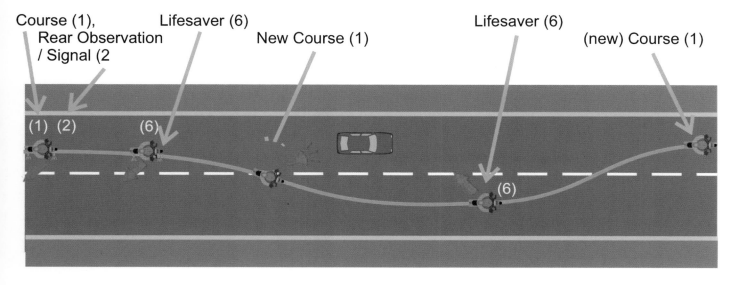

(Keep an eye on the gap between you and the vehicle that you're about to overtake.)

Make sure that you're in a responsive gear for the manoeuvre, in other words, don't have the bike in top gear at low speeds or else your throttle-response will probably be quite poor. In the UK, we ride / drive on the left so you should really keep your time spent in the opposite lane to a safe minimum.

This diagram shows the time spent in the 'danger zone' whilst overtaking a moving car.

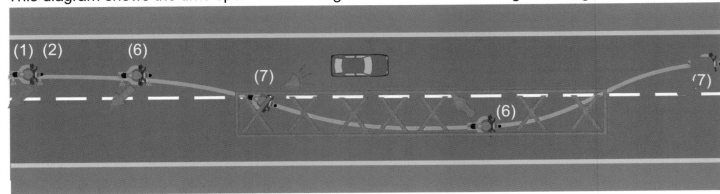

Shall we have another scenario ? This time, you're on a really straight road, travelling at 50 MPH and enjoying the sunshine out in the countryside. Ahead, you see a slower moving car and you also see that the road ahead goes slightly up-hill. At the correct time, you do your **Rear Observation (2)**, you switch your right indicator on and then after a couple of seconds, you do your **Lifesaver (6)** to your right and pull-out, just as you begin to climb the hill. Your bike is still in top gear and the engine begins to struggle half-way up the hill. Your speed slows. The car which you've just overtaken is beginning to overtake you on the inside. You're now approaching the brow of the hill, past which you can't see anything. You turn the throttle, desperately trying to wring more power from the struggling engine. The car is now directly level with you on your left-hand side. That's when you see truck coming over the hill at 50MPH. Game Over !

The '2 Second Rule'
At urban speeds, the **2 Second Rule** is an effective guide with which to keep a safe distance between you and any other vehicle you may be following. It's very simple to do and involves nothing more than counting the time between the rear of the leading vehicle and the front of your motorcycle using a static object such as a signpost or a lamppost (represented by the yellow dot).

As the rear of the vehicle In front of you passes the static object, recite to yourself "only a fool breaks the 2 Second Rule" or count "one thousand, two thousand" in your head.

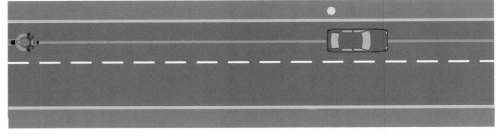

The front of your bike should not be passing the static object before you have completed reciting / counting.
If you find that you are too close, simply check your mirrors (2) (or do a **Lifesaver (6)**) and slow down slightly using the throttle and check again with another static object.

You should only be passing the static object AFTER you have finished reciting / counting.

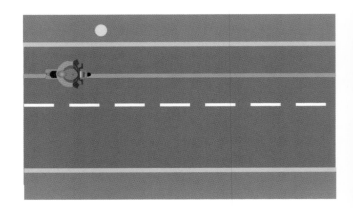

The **2 Second Rule** is only a guideline to help you judge a safe distance but the Rule itself is flawed at higher speeds, but we'll address that in greater detail in Chapter 7.

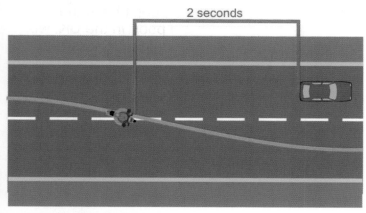

2 seconds

At no point should you break the '2 Second Rule' during your approach to the other vehicle, otherwise you might create yourself a whole lot of problems if the other vehicle brakes suddenly. As you approach the vehicle, watch for the brake lights which might mean that the other driver might be slowing down to help you pass quicker, or perhaps will suddenly turn right. If you need to, use the horn (two short blasts or one longer one) to make the other road user aware of your presence. As you can see straight-away, because of the car's course, you've had to cross the white line in order to keep a safe distance away from the car (at least a door's width). At higher speeds, a car can swerve at lot faster than a bike can so you'll have less time to react to any situation or hazard so you will need to be extra vigilant about what's up ahead in order to give yourself time and space. Expect the unexpected to happen, as always, which is why you need to be **Concentrating and Observing** at all times - **Riding Rule #1).** If there are no other vehicles to overtake, you can then start to think about pulling back in to the left-hand lane. The car may have accelerated, or there may be another vehicle (such as another motorcycle) coming up on your inside, so you will need to do a **Lifesaver (6)** over your left shoulder before selecting your (new) **Course (1)**.

Make sure that, in executing your manoeuvre, you don't force the other vehicle to break the 2 Second Rule by you pulling in too early.

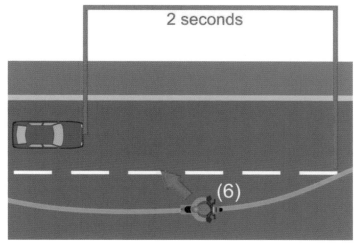

2 seconds

(6)

Whenever you overtake a bus, coach or Heavy Goods Vehicle, allow for them to have more than a 2 second gap to the rear of your bike as those types of vehicles have longer stopping distances, as this simple diagram shows :-

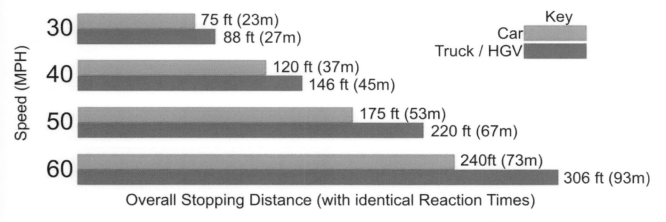

Speed (MPH)

	Key
30	75 ft (23m) / 88 ft (27m)
40	120 ft (37m) / 146 ft (45m)
50	175 ft (53m) / 220 ft (67m)
60	240ft (73m) / 306 ft (93m)

Key: Car / Truck / HGV

Overall Stopping Distance (with identical Reaction Times)

(Truck Stopping Distances - http://www.ukspeedtraps.co.uk/stopping.htm)

Larger, heavier vehicles are fitted with air-brakes which are far more powerful than brakes fitted to cars and motorcycles but the down-side to them is that it takes about half a second for the pressure in the brake-lines to build-up and actually move the activators.

If the other vehicle that you're overtaking is a cyclist or slower motorcyclist then make sure that you allow them room to wobble, avoid a pot-hole or be blown by a sudden gust of wind. Pass the vehicle as quickly and safely as you can - watch the speed limit - and be aware that if you double your speed (30-60 MPH for example), you will **quadruple** the braking distance needed. The Highway Code states that most people's reaction times are somewhere around 0.7 seconds, but the reality of it is that most people's reaction times are closer to around 1.5 seconds. Obviously, these figures are purely academic if you're not concentrating, not paying attention to what's going-on around you, not taking effective observations or are allowing yourself to be distracted. **Riding Rule #1 - Concentration / Observation at all times**.

Braking distances and reaction times are covered in greater detail in Chapter 4 but the graphic below clearly shows what a difference Speed and Reaction Times can make :-

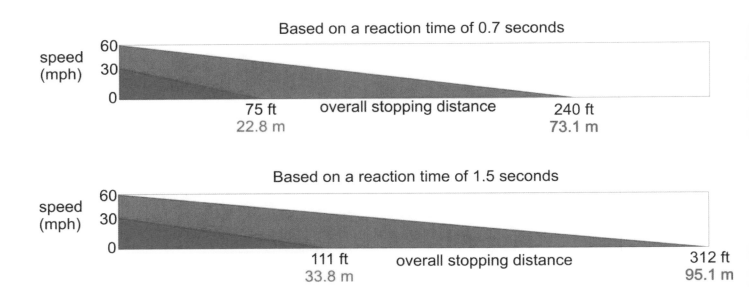

Your Reaction Times, like a lot of the skills needed for you to master the art of motorcycling, will become quicker with plenty of practice. An alert, experienced rider should expect to have Reaction Times of around 0.5 seconds, but that figure can be as low as 0.25 seconds. Think about what a difference that could make for a minute ... If you have Reaction Times of about 0.5 seconds instead of 0.7, then, in that time - at 30 MPH - you might be able to stop about 6 ft (1.82 m) shorter. It might not sound much, but that could be the difference between crashing and completing your journey intact.

You may have heard the term 'filtering' being used, and it describes when a motorcyclist rides in-between slow-moving or stationary traffic. Whilst it's perfectly legal to filter through traffic, you need to watch out for other vehicles which may be starting to pull out or pull in.

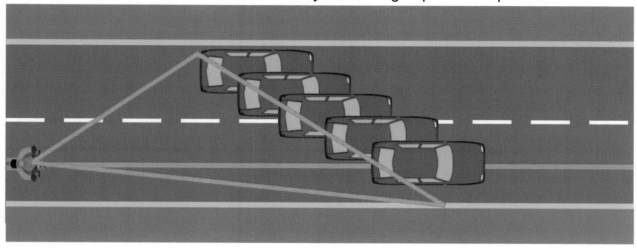

As you begin to pass the vehicle, keep an eye on the vehicle's front tyre to try to detect if it moves closer to the centre white line. Doing that will give you an indication that the vehicle may be veering or starting to turn right, or the driver is distracted by a mobile phone call, listening to the directions of the Sat - Nav, changing station on the in-built ghetto-blaster, (which breaks the Highway Code Rule #148) pairing a Bluetooth connection or fiddling with whatever other distraction car manufacturers perpetually insist on installing into modern-day cars.

Constantly scan the road ahead (**Riding Rule #1**) to assess any junctions, entrances, car parks, pubs, turnings or exits which a vehicle might turn into, or which other vehicles could pull out from. If you have any doubts, or an unseen hazard becomes visible, indicate left, do a **Lifesaver (6)** over your left shoulder and prepare to move back in behind the slower moving vehicle (**iiistds**) and remember to cancel your indicators.

When planning to turn right (up ahead) using a 'right turn only' lane, great care must be taken if you are joining other traffic, as the two lanes might be moving at different speeds. Filtering through congested traffic, or , will always have it's inherent risks but these are magnified when you have multiple lane travelling in the same direction. In the next example, you are in slow-moving traffic but need to get into the right-hand lane in order to turn right somewhere up-ahead.

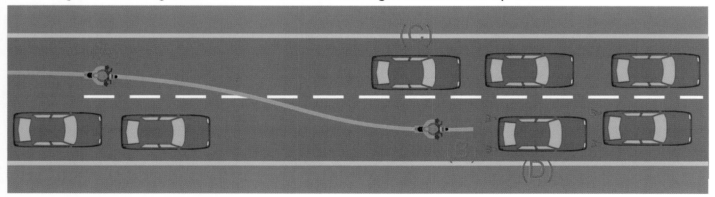

If you accelerated hard from point (A) to point (B), the leading two cars in the right-hand lane might break suddenly. By the time you would see the brake-lights of car (D), it would be too late to avoid a collision, with the blame lying directly at your feet (and head, arms, legs, hands and broken bits of motorbike !). Also, the car (C) could brake at any time, which would significantly reduce the gap during your bike's acceleration, possibly even leaving you with no room to even attempt the manoeuvre in the first place. We'll deal with acceleration and braking distances in great depth in the next chapter.

Let's imagine another scenario :-
You're riding along a long, straight road with very good visibility ahead but you then start to approach the rear of a slower moving vehicle. Decision time - overtake it or slow down ? The road ahead is still clear, as far as the eye can see in both directions. How many hazards are there, including the slower-moving vehicle ?

Can you see any bends ?
Dips ?
Hill-crests ?
Hump-backed bridges ?
Petrol station forecourts ?
Lay-bys ?
Junctions ?
Solid double-white lines ?
What are the performance capabilities of your machine ?
What can - and can't - be seen ?

You're now catching-up the slower moving vehicle ... Another decision - do you maintain your speed up or slow-down ?

So, we'll assume for a minute that you're riding along a nice A-road in the countryside well behind a vehicle which is travelling at the same speed as you are. But there is another vehicle in front of that one which is moving slower than you and the vehicle immediately in front of you. Keep taking occasional glances to watch the gap between the two vehicles reduce and that, by itself, will give you a good indication of when the faster-moving car will either pull out or brake sharply. Make sure that you keep a safe distance from the vehicle directly in front of you as the driver might not be paying proper attention to the slower-moving vehicle. DO NOT blindly assume that just because the faster vehicle could safely overtake the other vehicle that it will. Nor should you assume that just because the vehicle in front of you has accelerated, that it will be safe for you to do so. Also bear in mind that the vehicle in front of you might begin the overtaking procedure, but then suddenly brake and pull back into it's original position.

Never overtake when approaching a junction on the opposite, right-hand side of the road as traffic turning left out of that junction won't, necessarily, be looking-out for you as they will be more likely to be concentrating on the traffic approaching from their right. The same rule and reason applies to crossroads and staggered junctions.

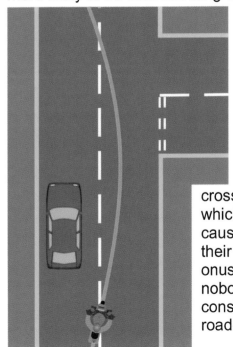

Whilst we're on the subject of where never to overtake, let's consider a few other situations such as approaching a blind-bend, approaching the crest of a hill, approaching a pedestrian crossing, outside a school or anywhere which would either put you at risk or cause another road user to change their course, speed or direction. The onus of over-taking lies squarely with the over-taker and nobody else. Just because a competent, skillful rider wouldn't ever consider overtaking in such dangerous places, always be prepared for road-using morons who will.
Prepare for the worst and hope for the best ..!!

Let's draw-up another scenario where you've just pulled-up at the give-way markings of a T-junction to turn right and you notice a bus pulled over at the side of the road, facing you, about twenty yards / metres to your right. The bus doors close, which would signify that the bus could be about to pull out into the traffic. Traffic to your left still hasn't moved since you pulled-up and as you look right again, the bus driver flashes his headlights and gestures with his hand for you to pull out in front of him. You haven't seen any traffic going from your left to your right which might possibly suggest that the road will be clear. The stationary traffic to your left doesn't allow for much visibility. How many hazards can you see ? Meanwhile, there's a driver who's late for work and is in a frantic hurry. The bus in front of the driver still has it's brake lights on and time is ticking away. The driver is getting more and more anxious, more impatient and doesn't want another grilling off the boss for being late again. The driver pulls out, straddles the centre white line and accelerates quickly pass the bus. Straight into the side of a motorcyclist who hadn't made sure that it was safe to pull out. That motorcyclist was you.

If you find yourself in such a position, use every technique that will give you an edge. By looking through the bus or coach windows, the overtaking car might have been visible and the accident would have been averted in the first place. If visibility in very slow-moving traffic is limited, apply the front brake, straddle the bike whilst being stood up and lean further over the handlebars allowing you look around the obstacle and get a better look to assess the situation.

Time for another scenario :- you are travelling along the inside lane of a dual-carriageway, some way behind two other vehicles. It is bright, warm and sunny. The leading vehicle is a 4X4 towing a large caravan and the car behind it has just exited from the slip road and is still accelerating in the inside lane. You're riding at a speed which is 20 MPH faster than the 4X4 is doing and you are already preparing to overtake it by taking a rear-observation and signalling. With the Lifesaver done and nothing behind you, you pull out into the clear, outside lane and accelerate.

Question time :- What happens next ? To make it a bit easier, this question is multiple choice :-

Answer A) – Nothing. The manoeuvre is completed successfully.

Answer B) – The car behind the 4X4 brakes.

Answer C) – The car behind the 4X4 continues to accelerate until it suddenly swerves or veers into the outside line without indicating, or checking first to see if it is.

The answer is : Any of the above, at any time ...

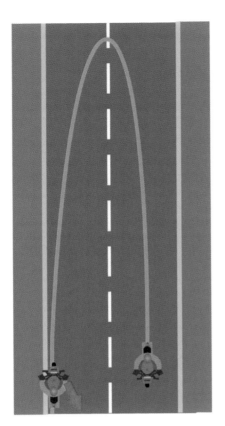

U-Turns are something which you may find yourself needing to do from time to time, depending on how good you are at getting lost. Obviously, it's a lot safer to do U-Turns on a quiet road or side-street, rather than a busy main road as you and your bike will be quite vulnerable during most of the manoeuvre. You will also find this manoeuvre at lot more straight-forward if you're used to riding at slow speeds whilst turning the bike.

On a quiet road, your manouevre might look something like the diagram on the left After pulling-into the side of the road (same as a left-turn procedure) turn your right indicators on, have a thorough look all around you to make sure that there is no traffic approaching from either direction before setting-off and doing a final **Lifesaver (6)** over your right shoulder. Then, balance the clutch and throttle and as you turn the bike, use a little more throttle and clutch to 'pull' the bike through the turn and accelerate away. Don't have both of your feet dangling or punting the bike round with your feet like an amateur - that's what the engine's there for !

If you are riding on busy main road, it would normally be suicidal to attempt a U-turn so you will need to find an alternative road on which to execute your U-Turn. If there is a side-road on your right, then simply carry-out a right turn manoeuvre, find a safe place to execute the U-Turn neatly, as described previously. Then it's just a matter of doing a simple left turn at the junction, which will put you back on the correct **Course (1)**.

If there are no right-hand junctions for you to use, then you could use a junction on your left, but that would then mean executing a right turn manoeuvre out of the junction, once you have completed your U-Turn, which may prove a little more difficult.

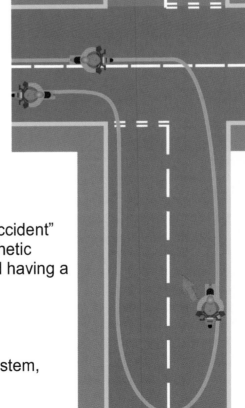

And that brings us to the end of the basic manoeuvres. With time and constant practice, everything you will have learned over the last few chapters will become second-nature. It might seem hard to fit it all in, at first, but you'll soon get used to it.

There's a saying in the motorcycling world "Good riding is no accident" and it's very true. Learning bad habits might be easier, an apathetic attitude to **Concentrating and Observing** takes less effort and having a poor Standard of riding might get you through a few miles but eventually, it will catch you out.

Remember, 95% of all accidents are avoidable, BikerCraft's System, which is based on the Police's 'Roadcraft', has a very proven track-record.

Chapter Four - Accelerating / braking / gears

Accelerating

There are several factors to consider before accelerating and comprise of road conditions, weather conditions, tyre conditions, your own knowledge and experience as well as the motorcycle itself. And you just thought it was a case of turning the throttle ?

Before accelerating hard, always remember :-

1)   Speed will get you into trouble far quicker then it will ever get you out of it at.

2)   All hazards (potential / otherwise) have to be assessed BEFORE cracking the throttle open.

3)   Only accelerate hard **iiistds**.

Road conditions will dictate the speed and if the road surface is loose and gravelled, rear wheel traction will be lost (you'll wheel-spin) if too much throttle is used. Rain will also reduce the grip available to your tyres as the treads try to displace rain-water. From my own personal experience I would say that the shinier and more reflective a road surface looks, the more slippery it will be.

Your experience of the machine, the bike's tyres, road conditions, weather conditions and visible hazards - as well as your state of mind - are all contributing factors as to how much, or little, acceleration you can safely use. The throttle will get you into trouble millions of times faster than it will ever get you out of it.

On a modern, powerful sportsbike where the rider is using too much throttle, particularly in the lower gears, the bike will have a tendency either to make the front-end feel very light or, at worst, 'wheelie' which is described as :- "a manoeuver in which the front wheel comes off the ground due to sufficient torque being applied to the rear wheel" (source :- https://en.wikipedia.org/wiki/Wheelie). Rearward weight-transference during acceleration is a perfectly natural, physical rule of physics but it's a force which must be used with great care.

In these examples, the red line simply represents the distance between the ground and the lowest part of the bike's frame purely to give you a point of reference.

A

B

With no throttle there are no forces at work but the more that the throttle is turned (A), the more power will be applied to the rear wheel. Through weight-transference, the forces at work will cause the slack in the bike's forks to be taken-up as it slightly compresses the rear suspension (B) but if even more power is applied the forces will cause the front of the motorcycle to leave the ground and cause a wheelie. With continued acceleration, the bike will 'flip' over onto it's petrol tank, seat, handlebars, switch-gear, mirrors, and seat-cowl, ruining them, and any other expensive bit of your bike that get's in the way of the landing ! Your bike's fall could be softened by you being between it and the ground, but I wouldn't recommend that as an option. Instead, I would recommend that you try and kick the bike away from yourself.

A wheelie can be prevented by not using as much throttle in the first place, but if you do find yourself in that position, slowly, gently, back-off the throttle and the bike will assume it's normal balance. Failing that, a light, gentle dab on the rear brake pedal should bring things back under control. Your initial instinct will, more than likely, be to grab a handful of front brake and there a 2 reasons for not doing that :- Firstly, your front wheel's not on the ground, so what good would it do ? Secondly, if your front wheel's locked as the bike lands, you're heading for a face-plant in the tarmac. Don't stamp hard on the back brake either, as that may cause the front wheel to land hard, probably causing severe pain in the genital / petrol tank area. It will also massively upset the machine's balance, possibly causing you another set of problems !

Always concentrate on what's going on, a nonchalant rider is nothing more than an accident waiting to happen. Generally speaking, a higher-capacity, bigger-engined bike will have much faster acceleration and will be able to go faster in each gear than a smaller-capacity bike would. Also bear in mind that it's a lot harder to brake during acceleration than braking from a steady speed due to the sudden weight-transference (see below).

Braking
Whenever you close the throttle or apply the brakes on a motorbike, you will feel an effect known as 'Forward Weight-Transference' which is caused, put simply, by the front forks compressing. The faster you go, the harder you brake, the more you will feel it. The effects of weight-transference will also increase if you are carrying a pillion or heavy luggage (tent / camping gear etc for example) because you are increasing the bike's overall Mass (weight).

Motorcycles are usually equipped with much stronger, more powerful brakes on the front wheel than the rear wheel because of Forward Weight Transference. As the front forks compress, the weight of the bike, including the rider, luggage and any pillion, is transferred to the front wheel due of the bike's Velocity and Momentum. Just like everything else involved with riding a motorcycle, it's all about balance. If we let the bike in the above example continue, we'd end-up with something like this :- (called an 'endo'.) As with flipping a wheelie, expect an expensive repair bill but also bear in mind that the bike won't be as easy to kick away so your body might end-up taking a battering ! The above diagrams show what would happen to a bike that was upright and travelling in straight line but that all changes completely if the bike was banked-over or turning. Both of these topics are covered later in this chapter.

Forward Weight Transference is the exact opposite of the effect felt during hard acceleration - Rearward Weight Transference. Under extreme circumstances, the rear tyre of the motorcycle might hardly be touching the ground, if at all, under very heavy front-wheel braking. Under those circumstances, the rear tyre is very likely to skid so it's probably better to take your foot off the rear brake pedal altogether.

For minor reductions in speed, engine braking can be used on it's own but further reductions will require the use of the brakes. Engine braking can, with enough space, be used solely to bring the machine to a complete stand-still by changing down the gears as the bike slows. If the road surface became extremely slippery all of a sudden, such as a sudden downpour, then the use of engine braking is a safe way of gradually reducing speed whilst maintaining full control of the bike. Under such conditions, hard braking with the front brake should not be considered unless absolutely necessary - Emergency Stop, for example..

As with everything else on a motorcycle, balance is involved in the shape of altering and adjusting the total breaking pressure being applied to both the front and rear brakes. Bear in mind that, as well as the weight of the motorcycle and anything that it is carrying, the forces acting due to Mass will include your own weight and the weight of any pillion. Maximum braking can only be achieved safely with the machine upright and travelling in a straight line. That's the point at which the machine will be more stable and therefore, more controllable. Braking, like everything else involved in riding a motorcycle, should always be done at the right time as braking too early for a turn or bend may increase the risk of traffic behind you trying to overtake or it might be travelling too close to the rear of your machine. Braking too late might cause you to skid and lose control of your machine. Everything has to be done smoothly and with premeditated fore-thought. Braking is a massive subject, so let's start with the basics ...

Generally speaking, on a well-maintained, dry road it is recommended that about 75% of the total braking force should be applied to the front brake(s), leaving the rear with about 25%. Before braking, the bike sits level as normal.

By distributing 75% of the braking pressure on the front brakes and 25% on the rear, you can see the forks shorten as they Compress.

For a good, but wet road, the figure drops to about 50-50, meaning that it will take you a longer distance in order to come to a complete stop. Bear that in mind when riding in the wet, or on wet roads. Due to less pressure being applied to the front brakes, the effects of Weight Transference will be less, meaning that the forks won't compress as much.

Obviously, these figures are just a guideline to give you some idea as to what it takes to safely stop a motorcycle. Trimming off a couple of MPH might only require a little bit of back brake use in some circumstances, but in the event of an emergency stop at a higher speed, virtually all of the bike's braking power (maybe as high as 100%) will be applied on the front-end. (Just watch for the rear of the bike lifting. If that does happen, simply release the front brake a bit)

Most of the time, you will probably be able to assess the road ahead, compare the potential hazard(s) against your bike's speed and pre-plan your braking accordingly but sometimes, you just have to stop as quickly as possible. An Emergency Stop is something that you should practice until you're perfect because when the need arises, you need it to be an automatic reflex. Each time you change your bike, go somewhere suitable and get used to how the bike performs under heavy braking etc., as all bikes will be different. Always have the bike upright and travelling in a straight line when you practice Emergency Stops, or else you'll be face-planted in the tarmac.

In the event of an emergency stop, make sure that the bike is upright and travelling in a straight line before smoothly applying pressure to both brakes in accordance with road conditions and climate conditions (50/50 or 75/25 etc). If you feel that you require even more stopping distance (not usually an option) then more braking power will be needed and the way to do that is to slowly increase the pressure on the front brake as you release the pressure on the back brake, until the forks are fully compressed. It is at this point that you can apply even more pressure to the front brake and the tyre will form a greater contact patch, but be prepared for the increase pressures travelling through your upper body and arms as the amount of weight transfer multiplies. The higher the speed, the heavier the bike, the stronger the brakes, the more Mass will be trying to rotate the whole lot around the front axle.

Notice how the forks go from being in their normal state through to being fully compressed. Once the forks are fully compressed, additional pressure can be applied to the front brake lever as you take pressure off the rear brake pedal.

Deliberately taking it to the extreme will cause the machine to 'Endo', which is the sort of riding best left to the professional stunt riders at bike shows and exhibitions, NOT down the local High Street ! If caught by the long arm of the Law, you will more than likely be charged with dangerous riding (Riding without Due Care and Attention or Riding without Proper Control of your Machine). Both Charges can carry a hefty fine and a bucket-load of points. The same Law, by the way, applies to doing a wheelie.

When approaching council-fitted speed humps in the road, ensure that your speed will be reduced sufficiently to be able to comfortably ride over the hump without you having the petrol tank thrust into your groin as the forks compress suddenly and bottom out, or being thrown out of the seat when the rear suspension suddenly decompresses. Try not to be braking as your front wheel starts to go over the speed hump because braking will compress the forks and then the speed hump will compress them even more. If they do 'bottom-out', you will - effectively - have no suspension.

The first diagram shows the bike under normal, neutral conditions, whereas the second diagram shows what happens when the front and rear suspension are both fully compressed.

Note the differences in the gaps between the tops of the tyres and the body of the bike.

Going down-hill on a road fitted with speed humps will require even more concentration as you should only be braking on the level stretches of road in-between the speed humps and you should give your bike's suspension Time to settle after braking in order to avoid over-loading the forks and rear shock-absorber(s).

Some types of humps don't fully cover the entire width of the road so, if possible, if it is safe and legal, then simply ride through the gap between the humps, but try to stay on the correct side of the road.

Skidding occurs when Friction is overcome by forces such as Momentum and Weight-Transference. Of the two tyres fitted to a motorcycle, skidding the front one carries the highest risk of injury. Skidding either tyre with the bike upright and travelling in a straight line usually doesn't cause too many problems, but if the motorcycle is banked over or turning, skidding the front tyre will, almost definitely, cause a 'total loss of control'. In other words, the bike will 'fold-in' on itself if you are turning, or slide away from you if you are banked over. Either way, you and your bike are likely to part company !

The first picture shows what happens when you grab a hand-full of front brake whilst cornering.

The rear tyre will try to do the same if the bike is turning or being banked over (as shown in this picture) so it's important, as stated before, NEVER brake during cornering or turning. During heavy (i.e. emergency) braking it is quite possible for the back tyre to skid due to Weight-Transference, as previously described, so make sure that you take that fact into account. Get used to thinking about how much pressure you should be applying to your brakes. Practice it until it becomes second-nature because then you will automatically know how to brake during an 'Emergency Stop'. Most people think that because they "nailed it" on their DVSA riding test, that they are brilliant at 'Emergency Stops', but that is a total misconception ! On your test, you know that the examiner is going to ask you to do an Emergency stop, probably on a quiet side-street, and you are ready for it. But in the real world, you'll rarely get any warning whatsoever, which is why it's called an 'Emergency Stop' and not a "Do It When I Give The Signal" Stop.

A similar result to the 2 diagrams above could also be achieved when the bike is banked-over and these are referred to as 'highside' and 'lowside'. If you use far too much throttle whilst the bike is banked over and the rear tyre begins to spin it'll do one of two things :- carry-on spinning or suddenly gain traction. In the first case, the bike will slide away from underneath you on it's side and is known as a 'lowside'. If you find yourself in this situation, let the bike go, don't try and hold-on to it. The second, known as a 'highside', results in the rider being violently spat off the bike, into the air, as the rear tyre regains traction. I'd suggest jumping onto your favourite video streaming site and learn from other people's mistakes.

Riding in the wet makes skidding far more likely due to the natural loss of friction which a dry road

can offer. See how shiny the road looks ? Look how clearly you can see the reflection of the bike's headlamp in the road-surface ! In weather like this, it's very probable that you will ride through standing water. Where possible, avoid riding through large puddles as you won't know what lies beneath - such as a large pot-hole in the road - waiting to catch you out !

On some side-roads and country lanes, if the road surface is renewed, most Councils will use a layer of tar over which they will pour fine gravel. You will usually see a warning sign like this one :-

A newly-laid road-surface will be littered with loose gravel which will act like marbles under your bike's tyres so ensure that you are riding at a reduced speed under those types of conditions. Probably the safest position would be in the outermost tyre rut as that is likely to have had the loose gravel compressed into the tarmac, or the gravel would have been carried-away by previous vehicle's tyres or have been scattered to either side of the rut. Allow extra room, between you and the vehicle you are following, for you to be able to brake safely, calmly and smoothly. Use engine braking and ride in a lower gear to give you better control of the machine. Do not panic if you feel your bike 'rolling' or 'wallowing' slightly as the tyres will naturally follow any minor contours in the freshly-laid surface. Also, do not panic if your tyres suddenly encounter a thicker pile of gravel at some point which causes the bike to slow slightly as the front tyre forces it's way forward. It goes without saying that the front brake should never be used under those circumstances.

One fact that does seem to elude most riders is that as the speed doubles, the amount of braking distance required to stop the machine QUADRUPLES. The proof, if any were ever needed, is in the Highway Code in the section on braking distances. If 20 and 40mph or 30mph and 60mph braking distances are compared with each other, it is obvious to see. This diagram gives a graphical view of that statement :-

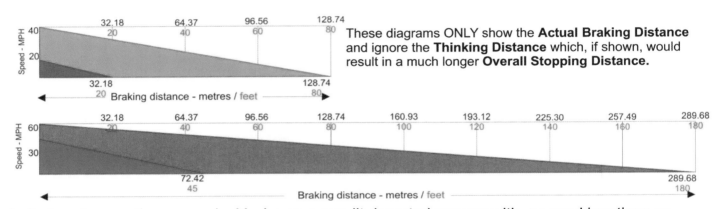

These diagrams ONLY show the **Actual Braking Distance** and ignore the **Thinking Distance** which, if shown, would result in a much longer **Overall Stopping Distance.**

Let's imagine another scenario. You're on a sun-lit deserted runway with, no road junctions or traffic, which has lamp-posts placed about 120 feet apart. Every single, possible hazard has been removed and you're riding along at 30 mph. But, as you pass a lamp-post on your left, you are suddenly forced to execute an Emergency Stop due to a previously un-foreseeable hazard. It will, with good reactions times, good tyres etc, take you around 75 feet to come to a complete stop. That's just over half-way to the next lamp-post. Now let's go back to the beginning of the exercise and start again except that this time, you'll be riding along at 60 mph when you then brake again with exactly the correct amount of pressure on the brakes, at exactly the same place. It will take you 240 feet, two more lamp-posts, to complete the emergency stop. Here's a bird's-eye view :-

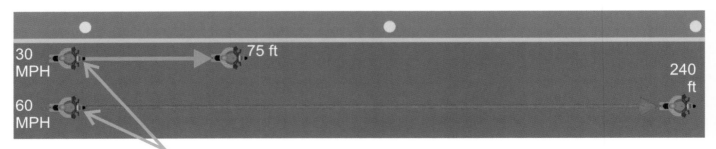

Both riders brake at exactly the same point, only the speeds are different ...

To further illustrate the point, at 20 mph it will take 1/3 of the distance between two lamp-posts to stop, at 40 mph it will take until the next lamp-post to stop but at 80 mph it will take you passed the 40 mph stopping point, with an additional two more lamp-posts and then some, before your machine will be stationary.

Let's really crank it up ! At 70 mph and with the Emergency Stop starting at the same time, in the same place, it will take you until just before the third lamp-post, but at 140 mph, it will take you about seven more lamp-posts before you will be stationary.

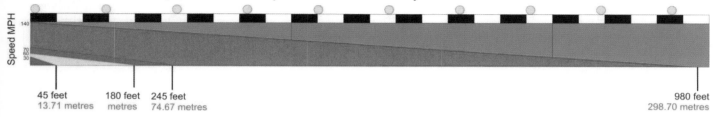

This graphic - which is drawn to scale - shows the differences in **Braking Distances** at 20, 30, 70 and 140 MPH, with each of the black / white boxes representing 44 feet (13.41 metres) and the yellow dots represent lamp-posts 120 ft apart. Remember, this graphic only shows **Braking Distance** ! To get an **Overall Stopping Distance** you will need to add-in **Reaction Time / Distance** and **Thinking Time / Distance**. Each block also represents the distance travelled in 1 second at 30 MPH, but travelling a 140MPH would mean adding 140 ft of **Thinking Time.** In the same amount of time, the bike would have travelled 205.33 ft (62.58 metres) - which means that you would have to add (just over) another 4½ boxes to the left-hand side of the graphic, plus another 3 boxes **Thinking Time** ! (making the diagram over 33% longer !!)

Perhaps this graph clearly shows why riding at very high speeds can lead to a prison sentence !

Some modern, large-capacity superbikes can accelerate from 0-100 MPH in under 4.5 seconds but would take 6.51 seconds to go from 100 MPH back down to 0. In that time, the bike would cover a stopping distance of 522.84 feet (159.36 m) - assuming good road conditions. good tyres, good brakes and an alert, competent rider etc. Figures from the TRL (Transport Research Laboratory,) show that a motorcycle can stop from 70 MPH in 245 ft (74.76 m). However, a motorcycle travelling at 100 MPH would only lose 29 MPH in the same distance, resulting in an impact speed of 71 MPH. This is due to the increased speed and, conversely, greater **Thinking Time / Distance** and **Reaction Time / Distance**, together with the fact that most speed is lost during the latter stages of braking.

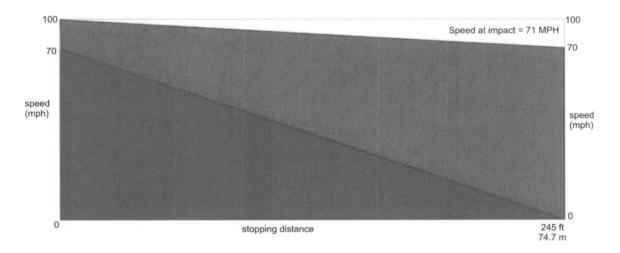

The next page shows the graphic from the top of this page, except it's much bigger ....

45 feet
13.71 metres

180 feet
metres

245 feet
74.67 metres

980 feet
298.70 metres

Speed MPH

140

70
60
30

Stopping distances are subject to massive variables such as the condition of the road surface, the amount of tyre wear and whether the road surface is wet or dry. However by using manufacturers tyre data and http://www.csgnetwork.com/stopdistcalc.html , it's possible to draw-up the following tables.

Thinking Time (seconds)	Thinking Distance	Braking Distance	Overall Stopping Distance
0.5	22 ft / 7 m	45 ft / 14 m	67 ft / 20 m
0.7	30 ft / 9 m	45 ft / 14 m	75 ft / 23 m
1.0	44 ft / 13 m	45 ft / 14 m	89 ft / 27 m
1.5	66 ft / 20 m	45 ft / 14 m	111 ft / 34 m

Its worth noting that 0.8 friction coefficient is the value used for *car* tyres when the tread is as good as possible and that the tarmac is perfect and dry. The first comparison table shows thinking distances at 30 MPH, a 0.55 friction coefficient values such as dry tarmac with motorcycle tyres that are 50% worn. (Distances are shown as feet / metres.)

So let's now look at what those figures would look like if it was a wet road, still at 30 MPH but assuming a 0.25 friction coefficient value, the difference wet roads can make.

Thinking Time (seconds)	Thinking Distance	Braking Distance	Overall Stopping Distance
0.5	22 ft / 7 m	50 ft / 15 m	72 ft / 22 m
0.7	30 ft / 9 m	70 ft / 21 m	100 ft / 30 m
1.0	44 ft / 13 m	100 ft / 30 m	144 ft / 44 m
1.5	66 ft / 20 m	150 ft / 46 m	216 ft / 66 m

Source :- http://www.csgnetwork.com/stopdistcalc.html

You can clearly see what a difference having faster reflexes would make to these figures. A novice rider may well have reflexes around the 1.5 second mark to begin with, but with constant practice, reflexes could easily be improve to around the .7 second mark in no time.

Wet roads mean that, not only will you will have to allow more time for your braking, you will also have to factor that into any manouevre or change in your road-positioning that you plan to execute.

Of course, these figures mean nothing if you're not paying attention to what's going-on around you. An alert rider will see a potential hazard far better than a day-dreaming rider will and can be ready to brake if the hazard becomes a real threat. Remember, **Concentration / Observation - Riding Rule #1.**

Avoid using the front brake at all if the bike is banked over or turning and there is a very simple way of demonstrating to yourself why that rule should be instilled in your mind. I accept no responsibility for any damage caused, whatsoever, either to yourself, or any bike if you practice this exercise but it will teach you in 10 seconds what would take 10 pages to describe. A moped or lightweight motorcycle would be more advisable to practice with, rather than a large, heavy bike fitted with panniers, a full touring fairing and a full tank of fuel. Take your bike off it's stand then stand at the left-hand side of it. Now, lean the bike slightly toward your leg, push the bike slowly forward (1-2mph), turn the handlebars fully to the left and then pull the front brake on sharply. You will instantly feel the forces, which act on a motorbike's suspension, as they try to 'fold' the bike over onto it's left-hand side. If you turn the handlebars to the right, lean the bike slightly away from you and pull the font brake, the bike will fall away from you, probably causing some minor damage in the process.

If you do the same exercise with the bike travelling slowly forward but banked over, you will feel the front tyre try to slide away from you. Whichever side you stand on, it will always fall away from you. When entering a bend or turn, always ensure that any and all braking is done <u>before</u> changing the bike's Course. Braking in a bend, particularly at higher speeds, will almost definitely cause you to fall off ! This could be caused by you running straight-on into the kerb / hedgerow / brick wall / lamp-post to your left on a right-hand bend, or potentially colliding with on-coming traffic on a left-hand bend as the bike maintains a straight line, caused by the gyroscopic effects of the front wheel. If you find yourself going too fast around a corner, a little bit of back brake can help but if that's not enough the 'Cornering' chapter will give you the answer.

Gears
Changing up and down the gearbox smoothly will become second nature to you as you learn the 'feel' of your particular machine. Your ability to control your machine could easily be Judged by how well the gear changes are made. Riding in the right gear at all times is essential to you having full control of the motorcycle at all times. Riding along in too low a gear will cause more wear and tear on the engine due to the higher revs, as well as reduce the fuel economy. Any engine braking will also be more severe with the resulting weight-transference being more increased. Riding in too high a gear will cause the engine to 'knock' and eventually stall. So, once again, it involves a balance between engine speed, road speed and which gear is selected. Town riding will require the use of a more responsive, lower gear but care must be taken not to over-rev the engine wherever possible. A good rider will know when a gear change, up or down the gears, is required. When riding up a hill, the engine may slow a little and if the bike doesn't respond well to the throttle, change down a gear (or more) until the engine becomes more responsive. If you're changing-down a gear, a well-timed blip on the throttle, just before you select the lower gear, will make things smoother.

You might need a lower gear for a lot of different reasons which will include :-

1) On an uphill gradient in order to maintain or increase speed.

2) On a downhill gradient where engine braking would usually eliminate the added use of the bike's brakes.

3) On the approach to a hazard, or where there is doubt concerning traffic conditions ahead, where immediate throttle response is vital either for extra engine braking or for accelerating away from the hazard.

4) When travelling at low speeds or when filtering through congested traffic. Again, immediate throttle response is vital either for extra engine braking or for accelerating away from the hazard.

5) On a slippery road surface where use of the brakes would endanger your safety.

Depending on the bike's engine size, layout and configuration, the amount of Torque and Brake Horsepower (BHP) it produces will vary greatly. The BHP figures will usually show a higher RPM figure than the Torque figure, that's just the way it is. But what do these figures actually mean ?

Here's a couple of examples :-
A Learner-Legal 125 will produce 12 BHP @ 10,000 RPM and 7 lb-ft of Torque @ 8,000 RPM, whereas a 600 Sports bike's figures will be around 132 BHP @ 14,000 RPM and 67 lb-ft of Torque @ 11,800 RPM. If we break it down further, these figures show that a modern 600 produces 12 times the power (BHP) as a 125, at much higher (+4,000) (RPM, and nearly 10 times the amount of Torque.

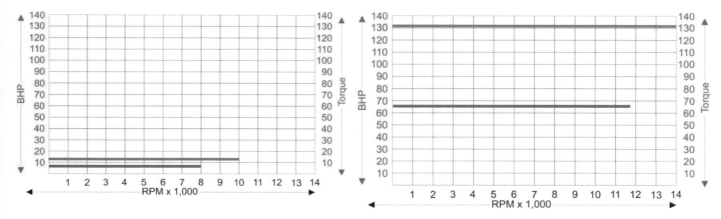

So let's now compare those figures to a 700cc Cruiser style V-Twin which produces about 73 BHP @ 5,000 RPM and 99 lf-ft of Torque @ 2,750 RPM.

You can see that the Cruiser produces more Torque at much lower engine speeds (RPM), but has a lot less BHP. In everyday riding terms, it would probably accelerate cleanly in just about any gear. This is the trade-off between BHP and Torque and these figures can help determine the characteristics of a particular bike.

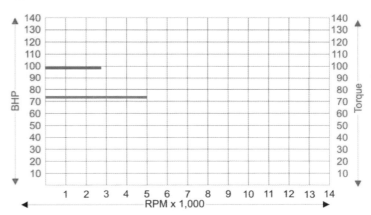

Let's now look at the figures for one of the kings of power, the mighty Kawasaki ZZR1400, which produces 207 BHP @ 10,000 RPM and 120 lb-ft of Torque @ 7,500 RPM. Note that the scale of the grid has had to be significantly enlarged in comparison to the other graphs.

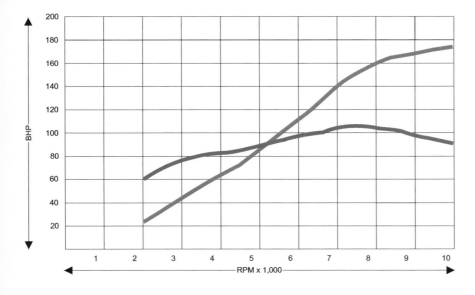

This bike would be able to Accelerate cleanly from 50 MPH to nearly 200 MPH using just top gear !

(Look-up the H2R is you want to see some mind-blowing figures.)

The type, layout and capacity of your engine will dictate your gear-changing. An American V-Twin, whilst similar in layout to, say, an Italian or Japanese V-Twin, will all have their own power characteristics.

All 3 of these bikes have V-Twin engines but that's about where the similarity ends. Each would deliver it's power in a different manner and, therefore, would be different to ride. Even if all 3 bikes had the same engine size, they would still 'behave' / 'feel' differently and you would need to learn how to best ride each one in the right gear at the right speed.

A Middle-Weight, In-Line Four, like the 2 examples shown here, will both produce different amounts of Power and Torque at different parts of the rev-range, giving each bike it's own style of being ridden.

Engine size (capacity) will also play a huge factor. A middle-weight, In-Line Four, like those shown above, will be totally different to ride when compared to a Large-Capacity In-Line Four like these :-

Again, different bikes will require a slightly different way of riding them due to their differing engines. Each bike will deliver its power differently, they will be geared differently, their Torque delivery will be different and where most of the power is in the Rev Range will be different.

Choosing a motorcycle is a very individualistic decision, so have a good chat with yourself as to what you want out of your biking life. Be practical with your options. If you're a young, newly-qualified rider you'll be limited by Government restrictions (and possibly, maybe, extortionate insurance quotes.) If you're a rider looking to take-up riding a motorcycle again, I would say this :- If you've been away for some time, you will have noticed that bikes have changed massively. In the late 70's, bikes were struggling to 'do the ton' (100MPH,) whereas any modern middle-weight Sportsbike can smash that, with room to spare. Modern road-going Superbikes are speed-limited to 186MPH. Spending a small fortune on the latest piece of motorcycling exotica will not make-up for your massive lack of experience, but it will least give road-hardened bikers something to giggle at, as they watch you wobble up the road. My last piece of advice would be to allow for the 'rose-tinted glasses' effect - you might not have been as brilliant a rider as you remember yourself as.

Observations

You wouldn't run down a road blindfolded, especially if you could run at 30 mph, as you know that you would certainly collide with something, at some point. The idea of BikerCraft's System is to increase your hazard-awareness, for you to be more perceptive in the identification of a potential hazard and to pro-actively react to any threats. Concentration is absolutely vital, at all times when riding, but be aware that sustained concentration will cause mental tiredness. Riding for long distances, particularly at high speed, requires a colossal amount of concentration which must be learnt through practice and experience. Similarly, riding through a busy town or city centre will require an equal amount of concentration, in a much shorter time and distance, if an accident is to be avoided. Never allow your concentration to be interrupted by any distractions whatsoever, otherwise you might not even see the accident coming.

Knowing what's going-on around you will allow you to better plan your course ahead. Watch for clues which might be able to give you warning of what is about to happen. For example, if you are following a bus, passengers might be seen to be getting up from their seats and moving towards the front of the bus. You can be fairly sure that a bus-stop is approaching so you can prepare yourself for either pulling-up behind the bus, or overtaking it in plenty of time, (**iiistds**), as in the example here.

By using this technique, you won't have to wait until the bus driver signals to pull-up at the bus-stop because by the time the bus driver even signals, you should be already prepared to carry-out whichever course of action you have already decided upon. As soon as you've dealt with one set of hazards, however, your next set of hazards need to be immediately assessed. Are bus passengers likely to step-out in front of the bus in the next few seconds ? What's the cyclist going to do then ? The bus is in a 'right turn only' lane, what if it needs to pull-out into the right-hand lane ? What effect will that cause to the traffic ?

You could be riding along in any town or city, with a clear road in front of you, and then something like in the photo below happens. Ignorant idiots (use your own words) can happen anywhere and everywhere. You cannot allow yourself to be concentrating just on what's ahead of you, you also need to be looking ahead-left and ahead-right, as well as keeping an eye on your mirrors.

The cyclist has no consideration for the rules of the road, however, law-abiding citizens have to keep an eye out for them.

However, it wasn't as if the cyclist magically appeared there out of thin air though, was it ? As I've said all along,

Concentration / Observation.

RidingRule #1.

An alert rider would have spotted this coming in plenty of time and would have been ready for any consequence. You might also hear "you came out of nowhere" as another road-user accuses you of this magic trick, but I'd take that as an admission of their lack of concentration.

The area shown in green on the right-hand diagram shows the extended range of visibility gained just by dropping-back a few feet and it doesn't matter if this was in the middle of an industrial estate, or out in the sticks.

 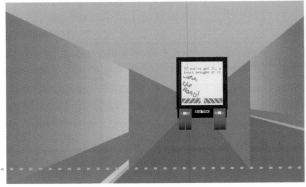

The dotted blue line gives you an indication of the extra visibility available just by dropping back a few feet. As you can see, there could have been a cyclist travelling down the road or a pedestrian waiting to cross, which you'd be able to spot ...

Use your observations to try and predict if a hazardous situation will arise but never make any assumptions. Again, when turning into a side-street, assess if any pedestrians will be aware of you, or if you will need to use your horn. If you see traffic-lights up ahead turn to red, then you know that you will probably need to stop. When riding close to the centre of the road, with parked cars on both sides, look through the windscreens and rear windows of the parked cars, look over the roofs, on both sides of the road, to see if a child or pedestrian is about to step out into the road. With larger vehicles, look under the front or rear of vehicle to see if any pedestrians are detectable and take whatever necessary, preventative action is required.

The phrase used is (Look) "OUT" -

which stands for Over

Under

Through

Observations must take into account three different factors :-

What can be seen ?

What can't be seen ?

What might happen ?

In this photo, you'd probably spot the on-coming ambulance with it's blue lights flashing and the red traffic light. But what else didn't you see ?

Did you notice the 2 cars exiting the junction up-ahead to your left, one's turning right, the other's turning left ? They've both stopped to let the ambulance past.

What about the elderly pedestrian waiting to cross the road ?

When following slow-moving traffic, especially in a town or city, don't simply watch for the brake-lights of the car in front as they will, more than likely, only be reacting to what is happening immediately in front of them. Try to watch what is happening three or four vehicles ahead of that, which should give you a little more warning of what lies ahead.

In just this one particular example, how many potential hazards lie in wait ?

The traffic lights are about to turn green (you should've spotted that) but you can't see past the bus. Is there another vehicle behind the white van turning right towards you ? Are there pedestrians still crossing the road ? What about the black car in the lay-by ahead of you, on your left ? Yeah, the one with it's brake lights on. Has it just pulled-up, or is it waiting to pull out ? Will any of the 4 cars in front of you let the black car out ? Will you ?

The above photo is just one snippet of the millions of snippets that it takes to complete any journey on a motorcycle. Under different traffic conditions, it might be perfectly safe for you to filter to the front, but not on this occasion. There's a bucket-load of hazards to watch out for in any given situation. For example, taxis or buses may pull out on you (with or without indicating,) parked cars may open their doors or suddenly pull out (with or without indicating,) cyclists may turn erratically without warning, or they might be blown off course by a strong gust of wind, motorcyclists, cyclists or scooterists might swerve to avoid hitting a suddenly-open car door or a huge pot-hole in the road, goods delivery vans and post-office vans might suddenly stop or turn, etc etc. All of these things, and many more, must be expected by the skillful, proficient rider. Some observations are down to common sense, such as if you see an ice-cream van at the side of the road, expect children to be running to and from it, but others must be learned. Take into consideration a child's perception of the road and think back to when you were a kid. How many times did you check for traffic when you were out playing with your mates near a road ? How many times did you just 'leg-it' to the shops, with pocket-money in hand, to buy sweets ? How many times did you chase your mate into the road and nearly got run over ?

Buses, coaches, HGVs and large vans can also impede your forward vision if you are following too close to the vehicle in front as in the example shown here, where the rider has placed themself far too close to be able to see anything !

Remember to drop back a little, so that you will be able to use your extended range of vision to check ahead for potential Hazards.

At places like petrol stations, supermarkets, lay-bys, local shops, car parks and public houses make allowances for the higher volume of traffic pulling in or out. Pay particular attention to vehicles exiting such places as the driver may not, necessarily, be re-acclimatised to driving. The occupants of the car might be arguing with each other, or are recounting an exciting tale to each other. Whatever it might be, expect that the driver(s) won't be giving the road their full attention and might not be concentrating properly, so you have to be extra vigilant. **Riding Rule #1.**

When approaching traffic lights, pelican crossings or other traffic-light controlled hazards which show green, never assume that they will stay that way, because the longer a traffic-light has been green, the more likely it is to change to amber, then red. One or more rear observations, depending on the environment, should be made when approaching a hazard so that you can be fully aware of what is going on around you and know what options are available to you.

When following another vehicle, it may stop suddenly whilst you are taking a rear observation so always make sure that there is plenty of space, and time, between you and the vehicle ahead. Remember the 2-Second Rule and don't be 'drawn-in' by the vehicle in front of you.

Whenever you pull-up behind a stationary vehicle at traffic lights etc, always allow a few extra feet in case the vehicle immediately in front of you the driver's brain realises what's happened and

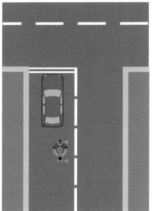

reacts to the problem, the vehicle might have reversed 6-8 feet or more. If you pull right-up behind a vehicle, as shown in this first set of diagrams, and that scenario happens, you'll wish you'd have listened to me more carefully !

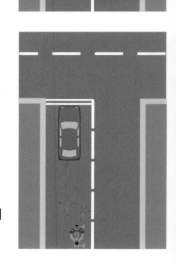

Simply avoid the situation by pulling-up a few extra feet back. Motorcycles are not like cars, you and your bike are the 'Crumple Zone'. Remember that fact whenever you pull-up behind another vehicle.

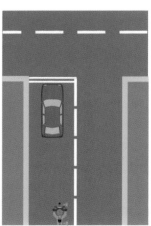

In this set of diagrams, the rider is far enough back to give the driver time - and distance - to brake. No dramas, no groin pain and no pesky insurance claim forms to fill-out !

In both scenarios, the use of the bike's horn might help, if only to attract the attention of future, potential witnesses !

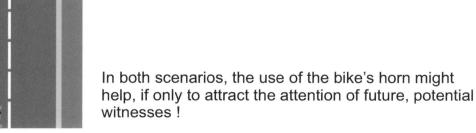

Depending on where you live and ride will dictate the kinds of roads you use most frequently and sometimes you might find yourself riding on sub-urban back-roads. These roads were generally built when not many people had cars, let alone parked them on the road, so caution is needed. Also, this might represent roads similar to where you might live so just bear in mind that 30% of accidents happen within a mile of your home. Familiarity breeds contempt.

In these examples, the diagrams show a bird's-eye diagram together with real-world photographs to give you a better idea of how to treat such roads. In the first one, we see a parked car which has to be passed safely but there's a sharp right-hand turn ahead which is 'blind' (i.e. you can't see through it.)

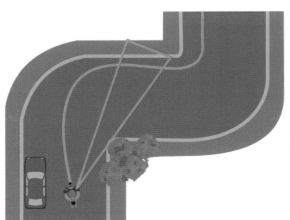

Did you notice the brake
Lights on the car in the drive ?
Is it parking-up ?
Or is it about to pull-out ?

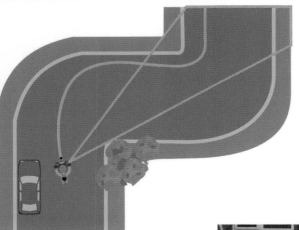

As soon as you've passed the parked car, move over towards the left-hand kerb (**iiistds**) to allow for any on-coming traffic but also take a Forward Hazard Observation to assess the road ahead.

Maintain that Course (**iiistds**), looking ahead of you all of the time to spot any potential hazards .....

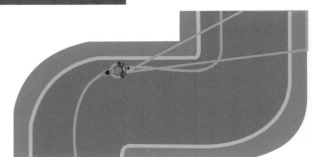

... until you are in a good position to see the road ahead and assess any potential or real hazards that may lie up in wait.

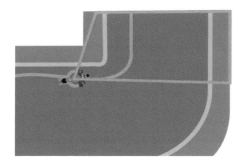

Just like right and left turns, for example, as one manoeuvre completes, another one has already started ....

So now let's turn around and do the same road, except the other way. As you can see, the hedge on the right is obscuring the view so you might have to adjust your speed slightly.

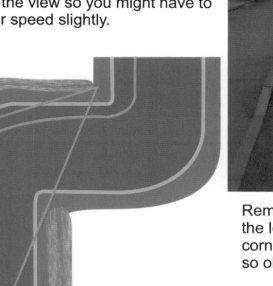

Remember not to ride in the gutters, but stay over to the left-hand side of the road. As you approach the corner, keep an eye out for hazards which may not be so obvious :-

Is there a driver in the car on the drive with the gates open ?

As you round the right-hand corner, you will be able to see though to the next corner, which is going to the left.

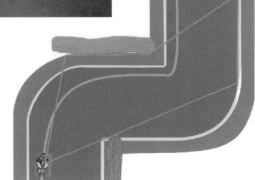

As you get nearer, your forward visibility will improve so make use of this information. Are there any parked cars ? What other hazards might try and catch you out ? Pedestrians ? Cyclists ? Kids playing ? Oil patches ? Man-hole covers ? Litter ?

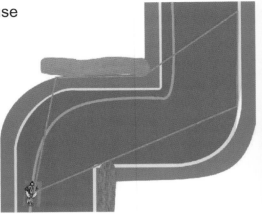

You're over to the left as you turn the left-hand corner, ready to assess the next set of hazards as soon as you see them.

Look O.U.T. (Over, Under, Through) both of the cars. Can you see a driver or any passengers ? Are there any other road-users ? Any erratic cyclists ? Children may well be playing in the street or on their drives but they'd be more engrossed in whatever they're doing than what dangers may be around them.

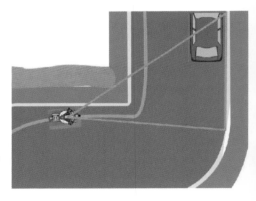

As with every manoeuvre, as soon as you complete one, you've already started the next one.

Positioning

Where you actually ride your bike on the road can enhance or endanger your position. For example, when passing a line of parked cars, give yourself as much room as possible by riding nearer to the centre of the road. Obviously, only if it is safe to do so and your manoeuvre will not endanger you or other road users. Watch for, and expect, pedestrians to step out from between the parked cars or for a car door opening. Remember the acronym :- Look OUT (Over, Under, Through) parked cars.

If, on a narrow road or street, there are parked cars on both sides then plan a course which will put you the same distance from both sides, assuming that there is no on-coming traffic. Always

ensure that you pass any car with at least a car's door width to spare, otherwise you may have to reduce your speed or even stop to allow on-coming traffic to pass. By riding in the correct position, by being further away from the hazard, your reaction time will be greatly improved. Always consider using the horn as early as possible as a warning to let others, like this pedestrian, be aware of your presence.

Road positioning can put you in less or more danger at any given time. Under some circumstances, your course might have to be readjusted to react to an unseen hazard. For example, if you are approaching a right-hand junction, which you plan to turn in to, your road position should be just left of the centre white line but you may need to move further over to the left if an on-coming vehicle encroaches into the left half of the road, as shown here :-

Similarly, with a left turn, your road position should be over towards the left-hand side of the road but you might need to take a wider turn into the junction so your position might be nearer to the centre of your lane. Cars parked close to junctions, or in lay-bys heavy pedestrian traffic etc might make the job that little bit more difficult.

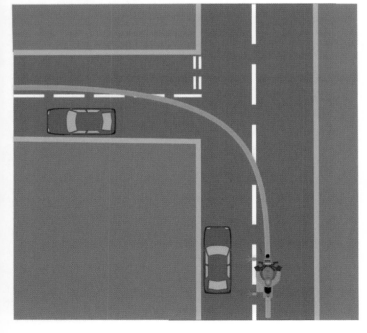

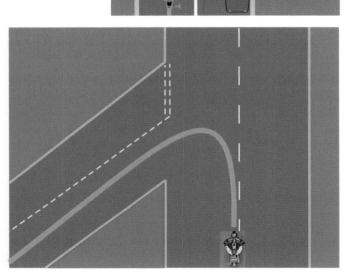

... or even an acute angle of the left turn are all factors to consider.

It's not just your positioning that you need to watch. Take, for example, a car apparently signalling to turn left into the junction that you're about to exit.

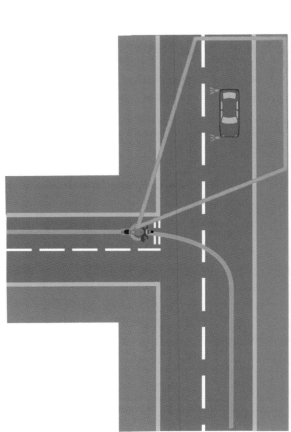

Just because the car has it's indicator on, you must never assume that the driver will turn into the junction. The driver may have forgotten to cancel it from a previous manoeuvre, or intends to pull-up on the left, just after the junction that you're wanting to pull out from.

The simplest, safest thing to do is wait until the driver actually fully commits to executing the turn, as shown on the diagram here :-

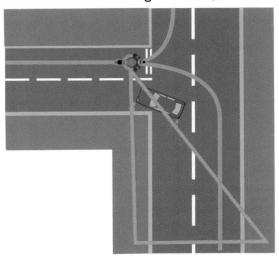

In this diagram, you're about to turn right from side-road and see an on-coming car signalling to turn right, or has the driver just forgotten to switch the indicators off from a previous manoeuvre ?

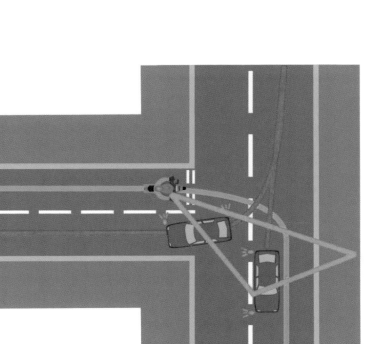

Again, your safest option is to watch for the car driver moving towards the centre white line and allow the driver to either complete the manoeuvre and turn into the side road, or carry straight on, before you complete your intended manoeuvre.

Make sure that you do a **Lifesaver (6)** over your right shoulder before setting-off.

Shall we have another scenario ? You're riding down a fairly wide main road, following another vehicle and you have already seen a side-road up-head, to your right. There is a car waiting at the Give Way lines and then the vehicle in front of you then signals to turn right. As it moves closer to the centre white line, you can see that there is plenty of room for you to pass it on the inside so you decide to maintain your speed and pass the vehicle on the inside as it slows down. What happens next ?

(1)   The slowing vehicle's driver changes their mind, pulls more towards the middle of the lane and accelerates.

(2)   The vehicle which is waiting in the junction of the side-road pull outs in front of the slowing vehicle and just misses you.

(3)   Nothing, the manoeuvre executes perfectly.

(4)   The vehicle which is waiting in the junction of the side-road pull outs in front of the slowing vehicle and crashes into the side of you, smashing you into the pavement.

Not surprisingly, the answer is :- Any of the above, at any time !

Here's an example of the scenario described above showing a bird's-eye view. The vehicle waiting in the side-road probably won't even bother to look for you as the driver will be concentrating on traffic from the right and watching the vehicle approaching from the left.

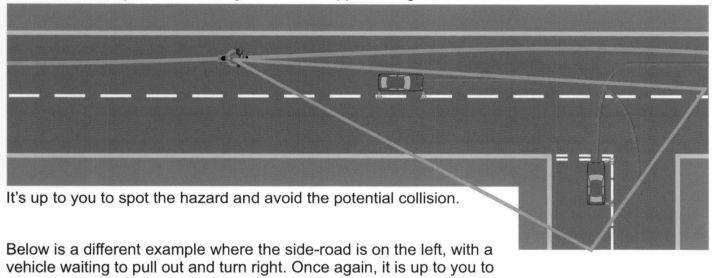

It's up to you to spot the hazard and avoid the potential collision.

Below is a different example where the side-road is on the left, with a vehicle waiting to pull out and turn right. Once again, it is up to you to spot the potential hazard before it becomes a real emergency.

Either of these situations might get even worse if the vehicle in front of you 'flashes' the other driver to pull out, even though that's not what 'flashing the headlights' means. (Actually, flashing of the headlights is meant as a visual warning, just as the horn is an audible warning.) It's no good being in the right if you're strapped to a paramedic's stretcher being carted-off to the nearest A&E Department !

When riding along behind a large vehicle, your range of visibility can be vastly increased by your position on the road. The following diagrams demonstrate the three different positions, and the corresponding view available :-

Whilst following at a safe distance, this represents the forward view if you were following the truck in the centre of the lane.

You need to have a better idea at what's up-ahead so that you can be better prepared for any real or potential hazards.

From the centre of the lane, and after a **Lifesaver** over your left shoulder, move your motorcycle further towards the left-hand kerb (**iiistds**).

From this angle, you have a good view of the left-hand side of the road and up ahead.

Here, a junction on the left can clearly be seen which would have, otherwise, remained invisible until the last millisecond.

About 50% of all accidents happen at junctions and by using this technique, you will give yourself a better chance by at least being aware of It.

To move towards the centre white-line, do a **Lifesaver** over your right-hand shoulder and move over to the right-hand side of the lane (**iiistds**). See the junction that's been invisible up until now?

Overtaking the truck, in this scenario, would be a stupidly dangerous thing to do because you already know that there's another junction to the left.

It doesn't really matter which order you look up the inside or outside of the just as long as you check both from time to time that you know what to expect up-ahead, as much is safely possible. 50% remember ...

In all of these drawings, the rider has only been moved sideways and is no closer or further away from the truck in any diagram..

Here's an alternative view of a similar situation as described in the previous set of drawings.

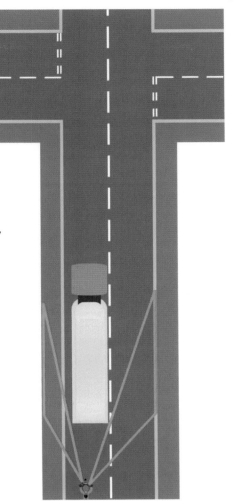

By riding in the centre of the lane, your view would be very limited by the truck in front of you.

By riding to the left gives you a view something like this:-

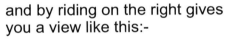

and by riding on the right gives you a view like this:-

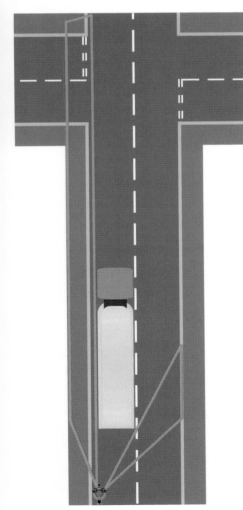

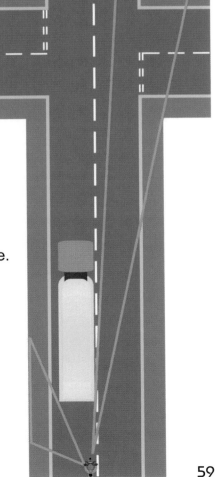

It doesn't have to be a truck that's impeding your forward vision, it might be a horse-box, a caravan or an inter-city coach, but whatever it is, this technique works every time.

Signalling, visual and audible

Indicators are there to advise other road users of your intentions and should be used accordingly. There is no point in indicating at the same time as executing a manoeuvre, the indicators are not there to let other road users know what you have just done. Indicators give a visual warning that you intend to pull out, pull in or park-up and should be given sufficient time and distance to act as a warning to other road users. Once the manoeuvre is completed it is vital, for your own safety, to ensure that the indicators are switched off. Make certain by getting into the simple habit of pressing the 'cancel' button twice, instead of once. Also, re-press the indicator cancel switch a couple of times a few seconds after you have completed your manoeuvre. You should not even need to take your eyes off the road to locate the indicator switch as it should be automatic, but if that's not the case, then you will need to practice until it is.

With the bike stationary and the ignition switched off, position your hands on the handlebars as you normally would and then, turn the indicator switch to the left, then off. Then off again. Turn on you right indicators, then off again. Then press it off again. Do it without looking, and then repeat this exercise with all of the handlebar switches, **especially** the horn, until it becomes second nature. In the event of an emergency, you will certainly not have time to look where the horn button is.

Indicating to turn

Your indicators are there to let other road users know your intentions but you've got to be careful that they can't be misinterpreted or misunderstood. Consideration and care should be exercised - particularly in busy urban areas - when planning to pull-up or turn into a road which is immediately after a left-turn junction.

In the example shown here, the truck driver might assume that you intend to turn down the first road, when in actual fact, you are intending to turn into the lay-by which is just after the junction (shown in green).

If you had your left indicator on at this point, your intentions might be mistaken by the truck driver. If anything, leave the indicating until much later but do a **Mirror check (5)** as you gradually reduce your speed, whilst keeping a vigilante eye on what the truck's doing.

Brownie points if you spotted the 'pedestrian crossing sign on the left.

Double Brownie points if you actually spotted one of the (green) crossing lights.

Arm signals, as described in the Highway Code, should be given in any situation where a reaffirmation would be of benefit to another road user or where you feel that you need to emphasise your intentions. In the event of an indicator relay failure, wiring failure or a blown indicator bulb, arm signals will act as a make-shift replacement. The other arm signal to consider and practice is the 'slowing down or stopping signal' as that is usually done with the right arm. Again, the Highway Code describes the correct way to give that signal which will also be necessary to use in the event of a brake-light switch, wiring or bulb failure. Pulling the clutch in will allow the motorcycle to 'coast' and therefore not too much speed will be lost during the time it will take you to give a proper signal. Once the signal has been given, place your right hand back on the throttle and re-engage the clutch safely and smoothly.

School-crossing patrols, Highways Traffic Officers, DVLA Officers and members of the Emergency services are the only people officially authorised to stop traffic but consideration must be shown if a member of the public is stopping traffic as they may be doing so because of an accident up ahead. Just because they are not authorised to stop you it doesn't mean that it will, necessarily, be safe for you to proceed.

The only other signal, although not mentioned in the Highway Code, is a 'thank-you' gesture. It could be an exaggerated nod of the head (you're wearing a helmet,) instead of taking your hand off the handlebars. Courtesy costs nothing and will promote good road manners and a better perception of bikers in general. If you are going to use an arm signal, do not ride for too long with only one hand on the handlebars as that could endanger you (pot-holes, Emergency Stop etc.)

The Highway Code describes the flashing of the headlight as a visible warning signal but great care must be exercised, particularly in daylight hours, as it has become the norm for it to mean 'pull out in front of me' or 'cross my path'. Both of those situations would put you at great risk if your intention of the signal was to warn the other road user, but their interpretation might be that you are allowing them to pull across / out. One method is to simply switch the headlight to main-beam during the potential threat, leaving your hands free to operate the clutch, front brake lever and horn button, if necessary. As soon as the threat is passed, switch the main-beam off. Never signal a pedestrian or other road user to cross-over in front of you with a hand gesture because if anything happens to them, you'll be liable in the eyes of the law.

A flash of the headlight can be very useful in the hours of darkness as a visual warning to others, and on faster roads, such as motorways and dual-carriageways, it can be used to forewarn other road users that you intend to overtake.

The horn is a vital piece of equipment and is used as an audible warning to other road users. However, the sad truth is that most horns fitted to the majority of modern motorcycles, even high-end sports-bikes, haven't changed since the early 80's and are pathetically feeble and usually inaudible within another vehicle. Perhaps consider fitting an after-market item from such manufacturers as Stebel, Fiamm or Hootaz which offer much louder products. There are no real, hard-and-fast rules (except Highway Code Rule #112) about using the horn, but there will be occasions when it's use might prevent or avert a collision or an accident. Even if you sound your horn, don't necessarily expect the other driver to heed your warning but, rather, be prepared to take further evasive action (**iiistds**) including an Emergency Stop.

Sometimes, even though every other precaution has been taken, the use of the horn would be justified and would include situations such as :-

1) As a warning to another road user who may be distracted or may not be properly concentrating properly.

2) Vulnerable road users such as push-bikes and pedestrians who may be about to cross a road or side-road.

3) On the approach to a hazard created by a physical feature of the Road, such as a blind-bend or blind summit.

Generally speaking, the more road users and pedestrians there are around you, the more occasions exist where you might consider using the horn. Also, don't forget that over 50% of accidents happen at junctions so use the horn whenever you feel that it will benefit the person (or people) that you're trying to warn. One short beep would let an erratic cyclist be aware of your presence, two short beeps might be used to let a parked, but occupied car, know you're there, two longer beeps might warn a group of pedestrians, who are about to cross in front of you, that it is not safe to do so. One longer beep might be used to warn another road user that they are about to create a dangerous situation.

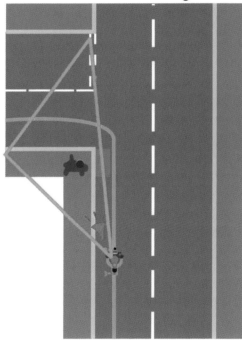

When turning into a side-street, observe - **Riding Rule #1 - Concentration / Observation** - the actions of pedestrians on both sides of the junction to assess if they are aware of you, or if will need to use your horn. By adopting a concentrated, proactive approach to identifying hazards, by using BikerCraft's System, many hazards can be easily avoided in the first place. The horn should never be used to let another road user know that you are angry with regards to their driving abilities ..... Or lack thereof.

Plan your Course / Speed accordingly if any pedestrians are going to be crossing the side-road by the time you get there because if a pedestrian has already started to cross the side-road, then they have priority (Highway Code Rule #170).

In this example the rider at point (A) is on a good course to be able to see the passengers getting off the bus so by the time the rider is at position (B), the horn can be sounded to warn the pedestrians of the bike's presence.

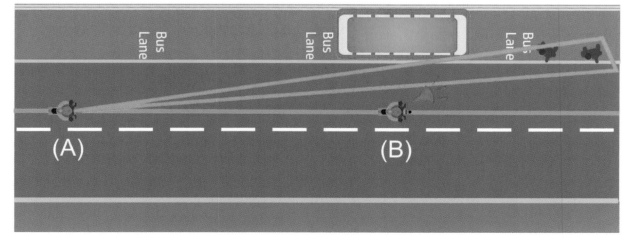

(A)   (B)

And whilst we're on the topic of buses, let's imagine another scenario :- You're riding along a typical High Street but in a place that you're unfamiliar with. There are parked cars to your left, there is on-coming traffic to your right and you are following a local bus. Before the bus driver even indicates to pull-in to the left, how would you be able to predict to yourself that there is a bus stop coming up ?

Think about it for a minute .... What would you do if you were sat on the bus and knew that your stop was coming-up next ...? Would you press the bell to let the driver know that you want to get off at the next stop ?

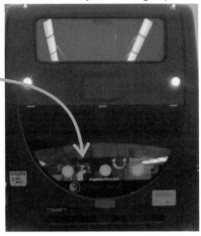

Would the bus' 'Stopping' sign be lit-up ? Would you get up from your seat, in plenty of time, and move towards the front of the bus ?

Use every tactic at your disposal to help give you the upper hand at all times, everywhere.

Directional Road signs

Apart from giving road users directions or local information, directional road signs also give you advance warning that potential hazards lies up-ahead because where there's a junction, there's a potential hazard. Remember, over 50% of motorbike accidents happen at junctions. In a built-up area, you should expect there to be more junctions with traffic speeds limited to about 30 MPH but in the countryside, traffic might be travelling at 40, 50, 60 or 70 MPH, depending on the road signs. And that's even if traffic is obeying the speed limit ! Traffic emerging onto a main road from a country lane won't be used to the higher speeds so it's up to you to make allowances for it and expect a slower-moving vehicle to pull out in front of you. In the example here, the two triangular warnings signs are clearly visible, and the approach to the lane on the left can be clearly seen.

But the lane on the right is partially obscured by the road-sign and hedgerow.

The road-signs warn of the crossroad but prior to these signs there would have been directional road signs who's colour would depend entirely on what type of road you're on, or are approaching. If you're following other traffic, be prepared for it to suddenly brake, indicate and turn - perhaps done in the same action. Also be prepared for vehicles indicating to turn, slowing-down and then suddenly changing their minds. 'Sunday drivers' (a term referring to dithering idiots who have all day to go nowhere) can be spotted on any day of the week, on any road and you're bound to come across one at some point. Patience will be required by the bucket-load and you can bet your bottom dollar that the minute you deem it safe to start an overtaking manoeuvre, they will do something, or somebody else will, that will scupper your plans. Cemeteries are full of people who couldn't have waited a few more minutes and bided their time ...

The next examples show a typical main road with a 50 MPH speed limit and I've placed the rider too close to the lorry in front. Forward visibility is non-existent. A vehicle in front of the lorry might suddenly brake, indicate and turn, causing the lorry to brake sharply.

Perhaps a vehicle might pull out of the junction onto the main road and cause the lorry to brake, or the truck catches-up to a slow-moving cyclist ?

Whichever way, you wouldn't be able to see anything and you certainly wouldn't have the time / distance to react to anything.

In this picture, there is a good distance between you and the lorry so you've got reasonably good forward visibility. You're able to see the warning sign on your left, and you can also see the first right-hand bend.

Major roads, dual-carriageways and motorways can be fast moving so it's even more important than ever to maintain a high level of **Concentration / Observation - Riding Rule #1.** Remember to use the 2-second rule. Keep an eye on your mirrors and take the occasional **Lifesaver** so that if you do need to make any changes to your Course, Speed or Direction, you will have a better awareness of what's going-on around you.

Let's now deal with Dual-Carriageways and how to treat both instances of slip-roads. In this example, you are riding along a Dual-Carriageway in the left-hand lane when you see the road-sign which indicates that the Dual-Carriageway ends :-

There is usually a distance marker underneath the sign, so if it says "300 mtrs", don't leave it until the last minute before you prepare to move over to your right. BikerCraft is all about getting everything sorted in plenty of time by identifying the hazards, assessing the risks, making an informed decision and executing your planned manoeuvre.

By taking Rear Observations with your mirrors, and doing a Lifesaver over your right shoulder, you will able to able to better assess the traffic in the lane that you are about to join. If there's no traffic around, then you won't need to indicate but if there is some traffic, use your indicators to let following traffic know your intentions. In this situation, you do NOT have Right of Way.

In this example, you are riding along the same Dual-Carriageway, except this time you are already in the right-hand lane when you see the same road-sign as before, except it's in the central reservation.

By taking **Rear Observations** with your left mirror, and doing a **Lifesave**r over your left shoulder, you will able to able to assess if any traffic on the slip-road is going to be a real or potential hazard to you. In this situation, you DO have Right of Way, but you should also be considerate to traffic about to merge lanes.

As a general rule, if <u>you</u> have to cross a white line, then <u>you</u> have to give way to traffic already occupying that lane.

A similar type of scenario can also be found in most large towns and cities, particularly at the start of a Bus Lane (for example) which might display a sign like this one (shown on the left) or similar to the ones shown below :-

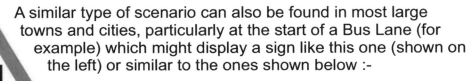

Also bear in mind that this type of junction is typical of where a motorway slip-road joins the main carriageway, except that on a motorway, you would, potentially, have the option to move over to the 2nd or 3rd lane (**iiistds**).

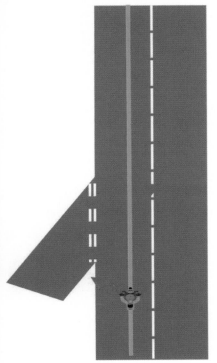

This would be the sign shown

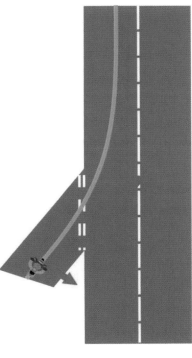

In all of these examples, the System used is exactly the same, with the only difference being that on motorways and dual-carriageways speeds can be much higher than in the Urban environment. Remember - **Concentration / Observation** at all times - **Riding Rule #1.**

Chapter Six- Cornering

Cornering

Exactly like a push-bike at slow speeds, a motorbike is usually turned using the handlebars to direct the front wheel, but at higher speeds you'll need to bank the motorcycle over. However, great care must be taken in learning how to corner as there is, usually, not much room for error. Before I introduce you to BikerCraft's System of cornering, let's get some of the jargon explained and we'll start-off with *road-camber* or *camber of the road*.

If roads were made completely flat, level and even then the chances of standing water after a heavy downpour would be extremely high so they are cleverly designed to disperse as much water as possible. The crown (middle) of the road is usually higher than the gutters, which are on each side of the road, and the camber is just the angle of the road down from the crown to the gutter. The angle is so slight that it is hardly visible to see but over the course of a few thousand miles, your front tyre (in particular) will show more signs of wear to the offside (away from the kerb) half than the nearside (nearest to the kerb) half. The following diagram represents a cross-section of the average road, going from kerb to kerb, with the crown of the road in the very middle and gutters on each side. The blue lines represent the direction of rainfall.

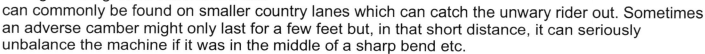

Obviously, different roads across different terrains will have different angles because roads are not something which are 'standard issue'. The phrase *adverse (or negative) camber* is simply used to describe a road which has a very steep angle from the crown to the gutter - or edge of the road in the absence of gutters - and is shown in the diagram shown here :-

Adverse cambers can sometimes occur through underground subsidence and can commonly be found on smaller country lanes which can catch the unwary rider out. Sometimes an adverse camber might only last for a few feet but, in that short distance, it can seriously unbalance the machine if it was in the middle of a sharp bend etc.

The opposite of an adverse (or negative) camber is a banked (or positive) camber and are usually caused due to the terrain. Many of Britain's most notorious roads have a mixture of both cambers and every type in-between, so be aware !

The term *apex* can sometimes be confusing, depending on what type of road it is, as it means a different thing on a race track than it does on one of Her Majesty's highways. As far as BikerCraft is concerned, it's the point at which you have finished <u>entering</u> or <u>negotiating</u> the bend and have begun <u>exiting</u> it. Here's a diagram to try to illustrate my point :-

Here's the apex

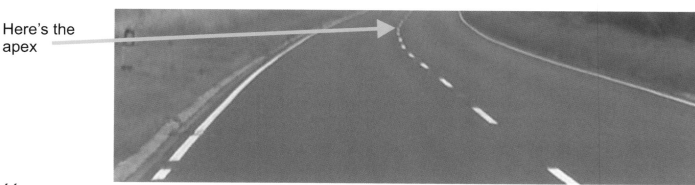

For riding in the opposite direction, the apex would look something like this :-

If this photo was taken in isolation, and if you imagine that the bend leads on to a mile-long straight disappearing off into the distance, then it would be a very simple manoeuvre and you could probably learn very quickly how to take the bend at a reasonably high speed. I want you to take a minute to just picture yourself learning how to take this bend (and the one shown at the bottom of page1 of this chapter.)

In the next example, the road appears to follow the hedge round to the left but, apart from that, everything else is pure guesswork ...

Do you think that it would be safe to go into this bend as fast as you would have in the previous 2 pictures ? How do you know what's waiting for you just around the corner ? You're out in the open countryside so there could be a car towing a caravan, a motorhome or a farmer herding his sheep or cows or he might be towing a trailer with his slow-moving tractor or be turning out of a muddy field.

In the example above, the apex might be another 20, 50, 100 or 200 yds / mtrs further round the bend. There might be a junction or crossroads ahead which cannot be seen for another 70 yds / mtrs. Then again, it might be perfectly clear and safe. This is where the confusion regarding the term *apex* arises. This is NOT the apex, it's called the '**Vanishing Point**' (VP), because you can't see around or through the bend, The road effectively disappears, and that's the next topic.

The term 'Vanishing Point' is self-explantory but just to be absolutely sure that we're all on the same page, here are a couple of examples of Vanishing Points. You cannot see past the VP, so you cannot be sure if the bend gets more or less severe. Or if there's anything waiting for you to crash into it, just out of sight ....

Some people might, mistakenly, refer to these as apex's but they might only be the start of a more severe bend ? Or the bend might suddenly go the other way, leaving the rider either in a ditch or on the wrong side of the road, into on-coming traffic !

Imagine being stood between two railway tracks. Through optical illusion, the tracks appear to 'meet' on the distant horizon and it's the same with the edges of a road. In this example, the VP is where all of the lines 'meet' with the horizon, even though (like the railway tracks) you know that they never actually touch.

But look what happens when there is a bend involved :-

The severity of the up-coming bend can be easily assessed by comparing the distance between the width of the road you're riding on and the width of the road as it appears to be, when looking at the VP. The shorter the distance, the more severe the bend.

In this example, I've placed the riders in a virtual world in which there is only one lane and no forward visibility except the VP. The rider cannot see through the middle. Effectively, the rider is on a bend that never ends, forever chasing the VP like a dog chasing it's tail. At no point can the rider see the end of the bend, so keeps out to the left-hand side of the lane for a right-hand bend :-

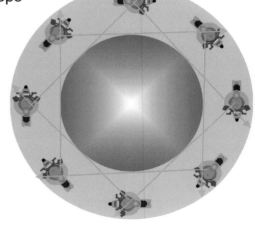

Or keeps over to the right during a left-hand bed.

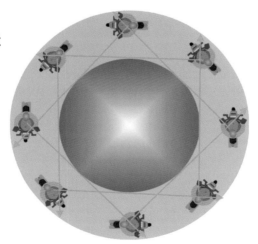

Either way, the riders will always be looking at the VP, waiting to see the apex and make the next set of decisions. The green arrow shows the point at which the end of the bend has been reached and the road straightens-out. This is also the point at which the rider can decide how much, or little, throttle to use, if any. There might be a potential hazard up-ahead. Or it might be a nice straight road.

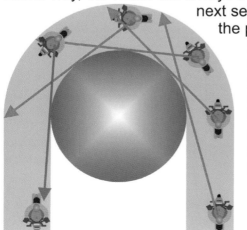

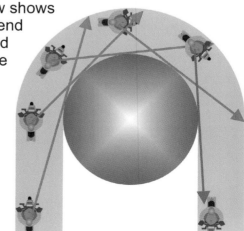

Let's bring back a couple of examples from earlier-on in this chapter and I want you to think about the different speeds that you would ride them at. Refer back to the examples of the 'line' (Course) shown at the bottom of page 66 and the top of page 67, then I'll ask you the same question...

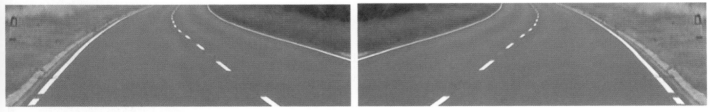

Done it ? Right, before I ask the question though, let's put the 2 separate pictures back together again first and highlight the Apexes and the Vanishing Points.   Don't get them confused !

Now I'll ask - How fast would you go, knowing what lies up-ahead ? Would your speed out of the first bend be slower ? Would you allow for Braking Distance into the second bend ? What's coming the other way ? Would you allow for on-coming traffic which may be driving close to the white line ?

Remember that you have to build your cornering expertise up gradually and remember that you must never, no matter how (over) confident that you might feel, ride above your limits, or outside the limits of the road, or your bike. Remember the simple formula from Chapter 1 :- High Self -Belief x Limited Skill = High Crash / Injury Probability. It takes time and practice, but always remember that your speed into a corner should be determined by how much of the bend you can actually see round.

There's another factor that you will have to take into consideration when dealing with right-hand bends and that is your own body ! Your bike's tyres might be on the left-hand side of the white line but, if you're banked over, your upper torso might actually be over the white line. If an on-coming car is also driving close to the white line, there's a very good chance that your body might collide with a part of the car, possibly throwing you off your bike in the process.

This picture shows a small section of a clear road with the green line representing a smooth Course through the bend.

But just imagine what might happen if a car happened to be here

at the same millisecond as you and your bike are ....

There's also a lot of scientific words and phrases which can be used, where cornering a motorbike is concerned, and these include Velocity (speed), Centre-of-Gravity (CoG), Centre-of Mass (CoM), Angular Momentum, Longitudal-Stability, Centrifugal Force, Friction and Gyroscopic effects. Each one of those words or phrases could (and does) fill an entire book so I'll try to make it as simple as

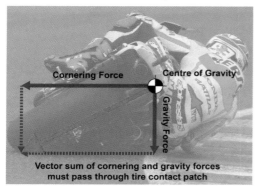

Vector sum of cornering and gravity forces
must pass through tire contact patch

possible. Before we start though, I want to make it **absolutely clear** to you that cornering a motorbike correctly is a craft that will take you thousands and thousands of miles of practice on bends to master. Racers such as those who race on the Isle of Man, or on an official race track have to spend years and years practising (and falling off) to perfect their art, to hone their skills. Most - if not all - of the Premier or Senior classes of motorcycle racers have dedicated their entire lives to the sport, so don't go thinking that it's easy, that you'll crack it in a couple of weeks, or with a few hundred miles under your belt, or knowledge of a handful of local bends. Because you won't !

Your bike's tyres are designed to alter their shape as the bike is banked-over so as to increase the contact patch - the bit of your tyre that touches the road. This graphic gives a good illustration of what happens as the bike is banked further over (the red area shows the increase in the tyre's contact patch). Cornering causes centrifugal force to press the tyres downward into the road-surface, compressing both the front

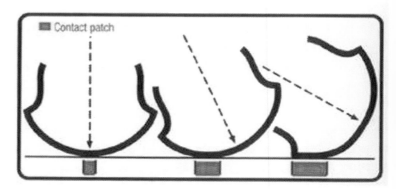

Contact patch

and rear suspension and reducing the bike's ground clearance. As long as there is tyre tread touching the ground, without some other part of the bike disrupting tyre contact, then the motorbike will still produce full cornering grip. The harder a rubber tyre is 'squished' into the ground, the more grip it produces. At a 45 degree lean angle, a motorcycle has nearly 50% more "weight" pressing the tyres into the road surface which provides nearly 50% more grip than it does when it is vertical, caused by centrifugal force. (Source :- http://genjac.com/BoomerBiker/Two%20Wheeled%20Physics.htm). Tyres are one of the most important components fitted to your bike - your life depends on them working properly - so make sure that you buy the best tyres that you can afford, look after them and keep them at the correct pressure !

Another fact to also consider is that as a bike is banked over, the rolling circumference of the tyre becomes smaller due to the decreased radius. In other words, the tyre is taller in the middle and Shorter at the edges, as shown in the diagram here :-

As you bank it over, you'll be using the shorter area of the tyre and the distance your tyre covers - per rotation - is less. This effectively means that a banked-over bike will lose speed in a bend if you Keep the engine at the same revs as before you banked the bike over.

If you're feeling Mathematical, here's the formula :-

20" Wheel + 3" (tyre height), Bike Upright = 26" Overall Diameter
20" wheel + 1" (tyre height) Maximum Banking = 22" diameter

Upright circumference = ∏d = 3.14 x 26 = 81.6" travelled per rotation
Banked circumference = ∏d = 3.14 x 22 = 69" travelled per rotation

Loss of distance = 12½" per rotation, which can amount to approx 10mph loss at "normal" cornering speeds, depending on the bike's gearing, wheel size etc.

An understanding of rocket science would probably be easier (and far safer) than learning how to corner a motorcycle but if you would like a more detailed, in-depth knowledge as to the meanings of the words or phrases, I would suggest that you look them up on web-sites which specialise on the technical side of bikes such as :- http://genjac.com/BoomerBiker/Two%20Wheeled%20Physics.htm, http://www.wired.com/2015/09/just-far-can-motorcycle-lean-turn/ or Wikipedia, as it's such a vast subject. It's something that you have to learn for yourself by starting slowly and building-up your experience and confidence. Learn the 'feel' of your bike, 'listen' to the 'feedback' that your bike gives you.

Different styles and engine capacities of motorcycles will have different characteristics, so always bear this in mind if you're riding an unfamiliar bike. A scooter will handle very differently from, say, a race-replica. A small capacity Cruiser / Race-replica / Tourer / Sports bike / Adventure bike / Road bike / Off-road bike will handle differently from a large-capacity Cruiser / Race-replica / Tourer / Sports bike / Adventure bike / Road bike / Off-road bike and it's up to you to take the time to get used to the bike. It doesn't take long to get used to a different bike but it's certainly worth the effort.

As your confidence increases, so will your cornering speeds but always be aware of the machine's limits, the tyre's limits, the amount of grip available and of any potential hazards that may lie in wait for you just around the next bend. Your bike might have had the latest and greatest suspension and tyres when it was new, but allow for wear and tear - particularly if you do a lot of mileage. Remember, High Self -Belief x Limited Skill = High Crash / Injury Probability. Here's just a few examples of different types of bends :-

(The green line shows the optimum Course through each of these bends. Note that there are no other road users to consider or make allowances for)

BikerCraft's System of cornering a motorcycle safely involves :-
1)   Correctly positioning the machine on the approach.
2)   Being at the correct speed for the conditions, and in the right (responsive) gear.
3)   Using the optimum Course / Line (see above) to give you maximum forward-visibility.
4)   Maintaining a constant speed and course until just passed the apex / VP.

Before you even get to the bend, there are several considerations to bear in mind. The first is that, on left-hand bends for example, there might be blind junctions, side-roads or exits which might require an adjustment to your intended Course (line). On right-hand bends, approaching traffic can pose a significant threat, particularly if vehicles are overtaking a cyclist on the approach, or during, the bend. In both sets of circumstances good, all-round observation is vital so that you will know, in advance, if it is safe to change your course or position. **Riding Rule #1 - Concentration / Observation** at all times. Is it sinking-in yet ?

Right and left-hand bends share the same technique which can be broken down as follows :-

Rear Observation – Before you alter your Course / Line, check that it is safe for you to do so by taking a Rear Observation (Lifesaver) over the relevant shoulder, or check your mirror, on the <u>approach</u> to the bend.

Speed – Using the brakes as necessary, make sure that the road speed matches the engine speed so that the throttle will be immediately responsive either for acceleration or engine-braking.

Course – learn to look ahead for adverse cambers and road debris, fallen leaves etc which may be lying in the road. Keep out of the gutter at all times when cornering as it will be full of loose gravel and litter - natural or otherwise - which could cause a puncture. There are basically two types of bends :- those that you can see right through and those that you can't see anything. What lies waiting around the bend ?

As you're assessing the bend, check if you can see all the way through it to look for potential hazards (including on coming traffic). Look ahead for side-roads, junctions or slow moving traffic. If you can't see through the bend, look at the VP and see how close the kerbs seem to get to each other as that will tell you how severe the bend is at that point.

Make sure that all braking and gear-changing is done BEFORE you start to bank the bike over, if you don't, you're only making life harder for yourself.

This type of road offers a far more open view, you can see more than just a couple of bends. You can prepare how you're going to tackle them as safely as possible.

Don't get carried-away on this type of road though as the nearest hospital is, usually miles away ... Let alone the nearest ambulance or A&E Dept ... (This particular shot, for example, was taken in the Southern Alps)

On tree-lined roads or lanes, particularly in the countryside, keep an observant, vigilant eye out for damp, cold patches under trees. The road surface could be just damp, or it could even be mossy if the sun never gets to dry it out and that will make the road-surface extremely slippery.

In the spring, fallen wet blossom will make the road surface slippery and greasy to ride on and in the Autumn, wet fallen leaves will also produce a similar surface. (And you thought only trains had a problem with fallen leaves !) Both are a seriously potential, seasonal hazards and are almost as dangerous to ride on as a thin dusting of snow is. Avoid riding on it where possible but if you do have to ride over it, particularly whilst turning, keep off the front brake and try to keep the bike as upright as possible.

When approaching a left-hand bend you should be on a Course which is closer to the centre white line but be aware of on-coming traffic straddling the line, particularly on narrow, twisty bends. Keep an eye on the road-surface but focus on the VP, constantly watch for any potential hazards which might show themselves when your forward view changes - which it will as you go round the bend. The objective is to maintain a constant course and speed from point (A) onwards with the bike in a responsive gear so that minor adjustments can be made using the throttle, if necessary. NEVER brake whilst the bike is banked-over. The best Course through any bend is one which puts the whole motorcycle under the least amount of strain whilst giving you the maximum amount of visibility. Continue watching the VP (shown in red) - from point (A) to point (B) - as you negotiate the corner, continue watching for adverse cambers and for any changes in the road surface or conditions and adjust your Course and Speed if necessary. Always make sure that you can stop your machine within the limits of your visibility. At point (C), the VP disappears as you will be able to see out of the bend and decide on the next course of action. Never assume that the road ahead of you will be clear of hazards such as slow-moving vehicles, stationary traffic or a badly positioned pot-hole. Or even a fallen tree ! Use your eyes to take everything in - **Concentration / Observation, Riding Rule #1.**

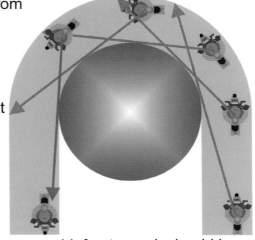

Hard cornering or accelerating with cold tyres when you're riding on a cold, frosty road, should be considered to be extremely hazardous and you must adjust your speed accordingly. Be prepared for, and learn to expect, unforeseen hazards which may force you to change your course or your speed. Never take anything for granted, expect the unexpected (as your instructor would have said). Your Speed and Course should otherwise remain smooth and constant until just after the apex - marked as point C - where you can then assess the next set of potential hazards and take the appropriate action as necessary. If the road is clear, then accelerate appropriately but if not, then you will have to decide on what course of action you need to take. You might even need to brake.

After the apex / VP, assess the road ahead and only accelerate if, and when, it is safe to do so. The bend might open out onto a long, clear straight or it might, just as likely, go straight into an opposite-turn, downhill, hairpin bend and you must be ready for everything.

To reiterate a point, take a look at this photograph of a real road and assess the hazards. What do you see ?

Did you see that the road bends to the right ? Or that there's a hidden dip ? What does the road-sign on the left warn of ? No fences or barriers means it'll be you versus the tree trunks if things go wrong. Did you spot the damp patches under the trees ? (The inset (bottom) shows a zoomed-in view.)

Damp or mossy areas. could cause the machine to wheel-spin if you're accelerating too hard. Unless the machine is perfectly upright and travelling in a straight line, it could cause the back-end to 'step-out' throwing you off the machine in the process. The same goes with heavy braking over a damp patch.

Never assume or take anything for granted, particularly on roads which you are unfamiliar with - cemeteries are full of dead idiots.

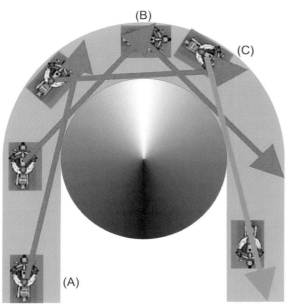

Right-hand bends share exactly the same process as left-hand turns do except that the bike should be positioned more towards the left-hand side of the road until the apex / VP (point C) can be seen past. Remember to stay out of the gutters. Other than that, everything else is the same. As with the left-hand bend, watch for on-coming traffic as you take the apex.

The apex / VP will usually be the first possible point of being able to see the road ahead, subject to the layout of the road. The phrases 'early' and 'late' apex are used to describe how a particular bend, or set of bends, is ridden and is determined by the layout of the road.

It might be more beneficial to take a late apex out of one bend in order to give you a better approach to the next bend. In this example, the right-hand bend's apex is shown here but by taking a late apex (wider Course or line) ...

... the bike is already set-up to take the left-hand bend on the apex

In this diagram, an early apex from the left-hand bend would mean that the bike could be stood upright sooner as you brake for the next 'blind' bend. All 'blind' bends have a VP, as shown here.

Being over towards the centre white line as you enter the bend will give you better forward visibility, sooner.

©Warren Photographic

Cornering, like most other things on a motorcycle, requires balance but unlike riding in a straight line with the machine upright, there are significant, extra forces to consider. The first of these is the Gyroscopic Effect of the front wheel which will try and keep the front wheel going upright, in a straight line. The hard bit, especially at speed on a large bike, is getting the bike to bank-over in the first place.

I take it you've seen the 'spin the bucket of water at arms length without spilling anything' trick ? Well, Centrifugal Force is the force that keeps the water in the bucket. Centrifugal Force and Gravity help to keep a bike stuck to the tarmac during cornering, as long as there is enough Momentum (speed) and Friction. Like I said few pages ago, a Degree in Rocket Science would be easier to fully comprehend but if you want an in-depth explanation of the Forces involved, may I suggest a visit to :- https://en.wikipedia.org/wiki/Bicycle_and_motorcycle_dynamics, because I'm just giving you the basics here ...

There will only be enough Centrifugal Force to act with Friction and Gravity if the machine has

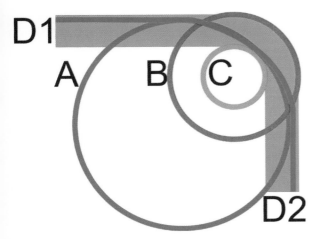

enough Momentum, but too much Momentum for the conditions, too much Centrifugal Force, or too little Friction, will break the grip between the tyres and the road causing the bike to slide away from you, as seen here on the left.

On a warm, sunny day, with the tyres at their optimum operating temperature, on a good road surface with a bike being ridden by an alert, experienced and observant rider, cornering speeds would be higher than the same bend being ridden by a novice, nonchalant rider on a bike with cold tyres riding on a cold, wet day. Speed is perfectly safe, but only in the right place, at the right time and in the right conditions.

This graphic clearly shows the difference that riding the correct line makes through an open bend (ie - you can see straight through it). Each circle takes the arc of the bend with (C) representing as if the rider followed the course of the centre white line while circle (B), shown in red, represents a rider staying close the kerb or gutter.

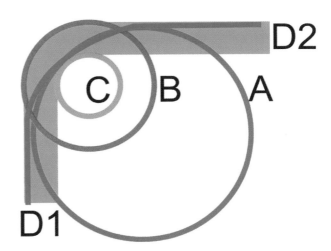

From point (D1), the rider selected a wide course, rounded into the apex and took the line back out again to arrive at point (D2). Circle (A) shows that this method of cornering places a lot less stress on the tyres because the rider using circle (A) could corner at the same speed as another rider using circle (B) or (C) but wouldn't need to bank over as much because of the larger arc. Another way to look at it is that rider (A) could lean over the exact same number of degrees but would be travelling at a much higher speed. This, by the way, is the secret as to how Police riders corner and it's widely considered to be the safest, fastest, smoothest way of cornering.

If the bike is going slightly too fast during cornering, it is possible to safely adjust your speed by gently, but smoothly, closing the throttle. As with everything else on a motorcycle, it should be done smoothly and in a controlled manner, not rushed, sudden or out of panic-ridden desperation. As you will have learnt, when the throttle is closed, the effect of weight transference on the forks will cause the bike's wheel-base to shorten. The resulting shorter wheel-base will mean that the bike will take, what is referred to as, a 'tighter line' due to temporarily shorter wheel-base. In other words, if you are going round a right-hand bend and need to shave some speed off, closing the throttle will make the bike turn more to the right. On a left-hand bend it will make the bike turn more to the left. You should never normally need to brake during cornering if you get it right in the first place.

Another technique to sharpen a bike's cornering ability - called 'Counter-Steering,' requires an enormous amount of experience, knowledge and practice but is one which is a useful tool to have at your disposal. Before we continue, I would just like to remind you about the disclaimer at the very beginning of this book :- "neither the author, nor anybody else however involved ... accept any liability whatsoever caused for any injury or damage caused whatsoever ..." If, after closing the throttle, you feel that the bike will still be drifting wide, you need to gently, very gently (!) push the relevant end of the handlebars in the direction that you

Push forward on left, lean left

Push forward on right, lean right

want to go. In other words, push on the right-hand side of the handlebars for right-hand bends, left-hand side for left-hand bends. Alternatively, pull gently on the right to go left or pull gently on the left to go right. Either way, your bike will steer sharper but, obviously, it goes without saying that this technique requires a certain amount of skill and machine control. Bear in mind that it only takes a <u>tiny</u> movement to change your course or position. The more you're banked-over, the more you will turn, but remember that you are never more than a couple of degrees away from losing it altogether !

What you're actually doing, during this process, is altering the aspect of the front tyre which is what causes the bike to turn sharper but bear in mind that you are also reducing the amount of tyre which is in contact with the road surface (the Contact Patch). Practice and knowledge will give you experience which will, hopefully, mean that you never have to rely on this technique.

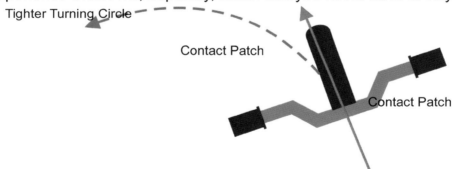

Tighter Turning Circle

Contact Patch

Contact Patch

If you get caught-out or utterly misjudge a bend and need to lose speed by braking then the only option you will have is to stand the bike upright, get it in a straight line and brake smoothly but firmly until the reduced speed is achieved. Realistically, there are only two places where that emergency manoeuvre could be performed with one being on the approach to the apex and the other being after the apex.

Once upright and travelling in a straight line, diligent balance of front-to-rear braking will be vital (under good conditions etc) and the method is to apply the front brake smoothly but firmly, with a little bit of back brake being applied, until the front folks are under full-compression. At that point, further pressure can be applied to the front brake as you take all pressure off the rear brake. Be aware that as you come off the brakes, the wheel-base of your bike will, effectively, lengthen and enlarge the turning circle. By lowering your CoG your bike will be easier to corner. Learn to read bends by starting slowly and building-up your speed as your confidence and experience grow.

Nobody ever got good at something by starting from the beginning going flat-out. Go out and find a good, short set of bends and practice the techniques described until it becomes second nature. You don't even need to do it all in one day and it would probably be better to try the same road every few days or every week. Start slowly, practice until you become more knowledgable, more experienced and then try it a bit quicker. Never try to exceed either your capabilities of the bike's. Remember the simple formula from Chapter 1 :- High Self-Belief x Limited Skill = High Crash / Injury Probability.

Knowing and choosing the right line for a particular bend is yet another skill which you will master with time and practice. There are no hard and fast rules as long as the basics are followed and that you always have your machine under full control without putting yourself or anybody else at risk. Never let your enthusiasm exceed your capabilities or the conditions. Expect the unexpected, particularly when cornering and be ready to sound the horn should the need arise. Use of the horn should also be considered if you're approaching a tight, hair-pin bend and you

might need to reduce your speed so that you can stop within the visible distance available to you.

The amount of acceleration will depend on factors such as visible hazards, the road surface, tyre condition and temperature, other road users, climate conditions and the physical layout of the road such as adverse cambers or hills. On the subject of Acceleration, let's bring back the 30-60 and 70-140 MPH Braking Distance graph to remind you that if you double your speed, you quadruple your Braking Distance !

| 45 feet 13.71 metres | 180 feet metres | 245 feet 74.67 metres | 980 feet 298.70 metres |

When descending a hill, keep the bike in a low gear and gently use the back brake, after the apex, if necessary. Try to avoid using the front brakes unless the bike is upright and travelling in a straight line.

Never try to emulate your race-track hero on the public roads. For a start, race-tracks are much wider than most public roads, have a better surface than most public roads and are designed specifically for one purpose. Most public roads are two-way and have a vast mixture of vehicles, any of which could turn, pull-out, slow down or stop suddenly and without warning in front of you. Not to mention other immediate hazards such as bollards, solid centre white lines, man-hole covers, cat's eyes, pelican crossings, junctions, traffic lights, pedestrians and speed limits. And traffic coppers, police helicopters, police spotter-planes, average speed cameras and Gatsos. If you are caught racing on the Highway, you will be charged under Code MS50 and land yourself with between 3 and 11 points on your licence, plus a very hefty fine. Plus the points / fine for Speeding (SP30, 3-6 points) or Dangerous Driving (DD40, 3-11 points) etc ...

Accident 'Black-spots' are commonly found on long, straight stretches of road but even more so where there is also a bend involved. Any idiot can turn a throttle or press an accelerator to go fast, but it takes an experienced, skilled driver or rider to do so safely at higher speeds. An inexperienced rider (or driver) will not be able to perceive or understand the forces which will act upon the vehicle, nor will they be able to assess that they are going too fast until it's far too late. Knowing how to read the road, knowing your machine's capabilities, knowing it's limits and knowing how to use the safest, smoothest, fastest line through any bend will make you a better, safer and more competent rider.

A vehicle parked on the entry to a tight right-hand bend would pose a far more significant risk than one parked in the same place on the approach to a left-hand bend. However, approach speed, passing speed, clearance distance (between you and the parked car) and low gear selection will all have to be taken into consideration when negotiating the parked car on the approach to the bend. As will any on-coming traffic, so have your fingers ready over the front brake lever and have your foot over the rear brake pedal - just in case.

In the right-bend scenario, the vehicle would mean that you would have to move further over towards the centre white line on the approach to the bend, potentially increasing the risk of colliding with on-coming traffic due to the lack of forward vision. In the left-hand bend scenario, your natural course would be over towards the centre white line in order to obtain the maximum view ahead, well away from the parked vehicle, until just after the apex.

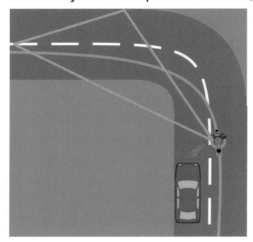
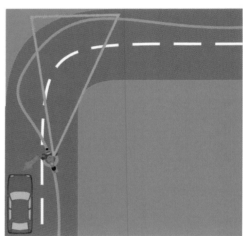

Angles of lean will vary dependent on the road's surface and condition, climate conditions, forward view, presence of hazards, the severity of the bend, the width of the road, the length of the bend, the speed at which you are travelling, your experience and the bike itself.

Here's a couple of typical examples of the types of roads that you might encounter and with good forward visibility you could corner on the apexes

... rather than just after them, as shown by the green lines. Did you notice that one road goes slightly down-hill and one goes slightly up-hill ? You will need to adjust the amount of acceleration or deceleration accordingly, which is where being in the right gear at the right speed and in the correct road position will prove - time and time again - to be beneficial to you. In a nut-shell, cornering is about Visibility, Course, Speed and Gear. If you get those 4 things right, you'll be well on your way to mastering Cornering.

In this picture, your Course / line would need to be so that your bike is positioned out towards the left-hand side of the road - just before the road disappears - in order to give yourself the maximum visibility around the bend. This particular line has had to be adjusted slightly in order to avoid the loose dirt and the man-hole cover, both of which could pose a potential hazard unless the bike is upright and travelling in a straight line, particularly in wet conditions.

These two pictures are very similar types of bend, except In the picture below, you are able to use the entire width of the lane, with good forward visibility, on a reasonably good road surface and in good weather ...

.. but take a look at the picture below. There's a slow-moving tractor with a queue of cars following it in the opposite lane and hatch markings across the middle of the road. Could an impatient driver try to overtake the tractor ? There's a fairly sharp right hand bend coming up which is shaded under the trees. Might the road be damp and slippery in places ? What's around the bend ?

Did you notice the 'SLOW' road marking ? That would tell you that there's a potential, unseen hazard lying in wait ...

Concentration / Observation - Riding Rule #1.

There are a lot of videos on the 'net which are posted by people who only seem to use about a quarter of the lane, instead of the whole width of the lane, or even the road. This is a riding style which has it's limits, and could even be counter-productive.

This diagram shows what I mean :-

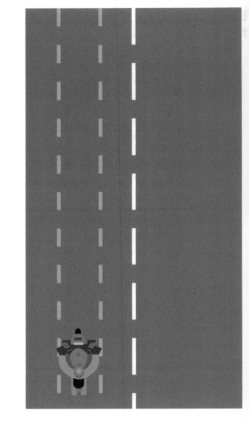

In order for me to give you some idea, the diagram below clearly showing the advantage of correct positioning when entering a bend.:-

The view through the bend is obscured by the trees for the rider on the left of the lane, whereas the rider on the right-hand side of the lane would be able to see the HGV and take whatever action would be necessary.

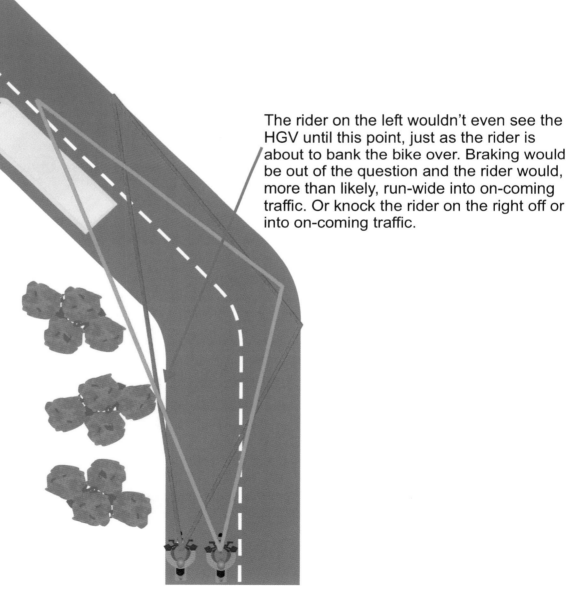

The rider on the left wouldn't even see the HGV until this point, just as the rider is about to bank the bike over. Braking would be out of the question and the rider would, more than likely, run-wide into on-coming traffic. Or knock the rider on the right off or into on-coming traffic.

Let's compare 2 different riders on the same set of bends, same bike etc, at the same entry speed for the first bend.

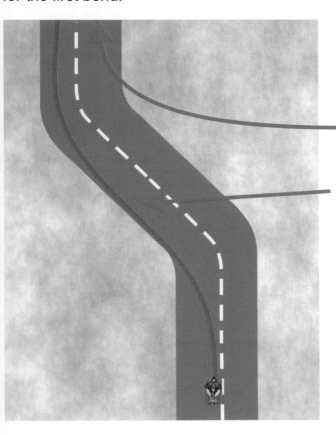

In this example, the rider is on a perfect Course, riding just to the left of the centre line and has good forward visibility. By taking this Course, the bike is hardly banked over and the rider has made sure that the speed is appropriate and that he bike is in the correct gear.

If the road after here suddenly went into a sharp left or right-hand bend, any further braking could be done on the short straight between the two bends whilst the bike is upright and travelling in a straight line..

This diagram shows what happens if the rider enters the bend slightly too fast. Don't forget that both of the riders in these diagrams are approaching the first bend at exactly the same speed. The only difference is road positioning.

The rider here is positioned more over to the left-hand side of the lane entering the first left-hand bend.

Due to the speed of the bike, the curvature of the road, CoG, CoM, Centrifugal Force and the Gyroscopic Effect, the rider shown here would be forced out towards the centre of the road. It's too late to brake and, unlike the previous example, there's nowhere to straighten-up the bike and brake.

Panic will probably set-in, the rider will, likely, just 'freeze' and hope for the best.

The red lines show the possible crash-sites.

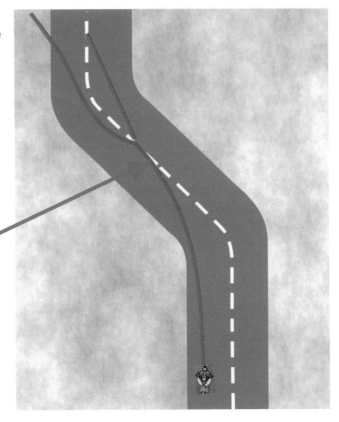

Accidents on bends are usually because the rider has totally failed to 'read' the road ahead properly, or isn't fully concentrating, There are many examples on the 'net (search :- Motorcycle crash, for example) which show a rider 'losing it.' I would suggest that you spend some time learning from other people's mistakes, rather than make all of your own !

In a nutshell, at lease one of these factors is usually the cause ;-

> Entry Speed is too fast.
> Use of the front brake.
> Too much throttle at the Apex.
> Assuming that the road straightens-out after the VP.
> Failing to Bank the bike over properly.
> Failure to use the correct Course.

Entry Speed is too fast
Going into a bend too fast is an example of exceeding your abilities. It might be a bend that you know, but at higher speeds your bike will handle very differently. Take the time to 'learn' your bike and the bend(s).

Use of the front brake
Unless the bike is upright and travelling in a straight line, the rules are simple - DON'T !

Too much throttle at the Apex
Also known as 'High-siding' in the race-track world and starts with the rear tyre spinning. The problems start when the tyre gains traction again, usually resulting in the rider being catapulted off very violently.

Assuming that the road straightens-out after the first VP
They seem to assume that what they can see is the apex, but it's actually the VP, only the start of the turn, and is a classic mistake. If the road bends to the left, the rider will have no choice but to veer into the opposite lane. All it'll take is 1 vehicle coming the other way .... If the road bends round to the right, then anything like a wall, hedge, lamp-post, telegraph pole or 40ft drop will soon spoil your day.

Failing to Bank the bike over properly
The faster you navigate a particular bend, the further over you'll need to bank your bike. Also, if you're carrying a pillion and / or luggage, the same rule applies. Take the time to learn.

Failure to use the correct Course
As previously explained, your Course must make the most of the layout of the road and is the most important thing to get right, after your Entry Speed.

Now let's put that into a graphic with all riders at the same Entry Speed, on a bend which is based on a real section of road. The particular section which I've chosen is where the road is cut into a large hill on your left-hand side, so there's very limited Forward / Left visibility. Oh, and there's also a sheer drop on the other side of the road :-

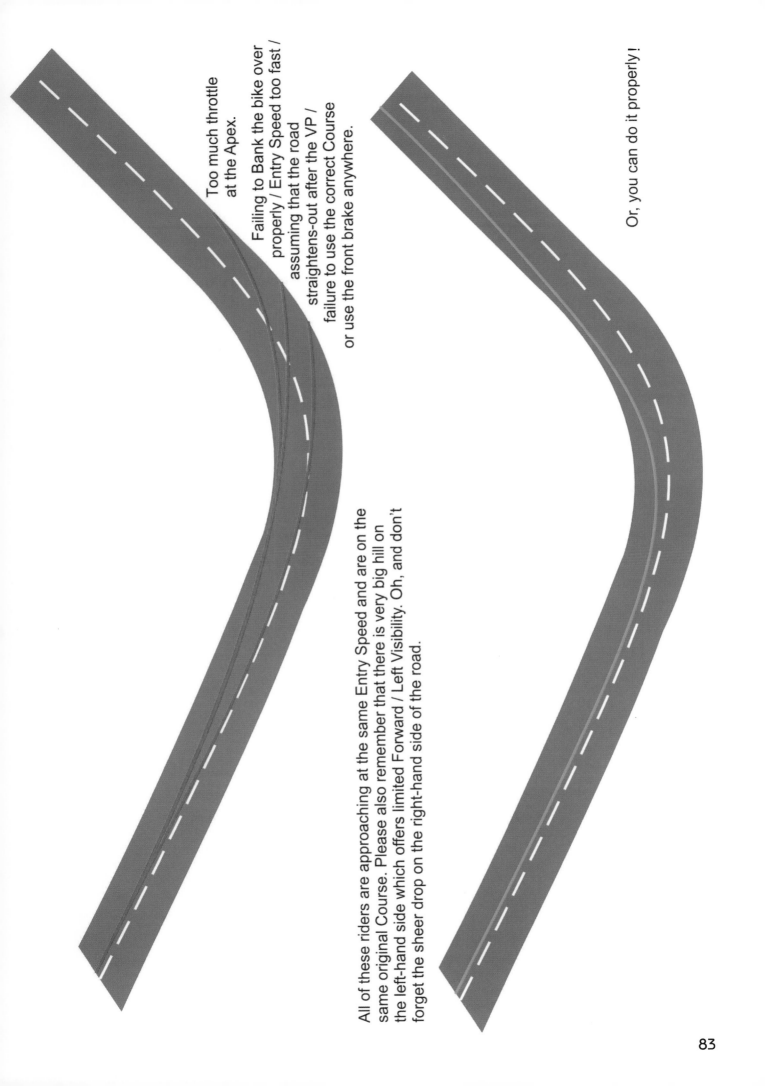

Too much throttle at the Apex.

Failing to Bank the bike over properly / Entry Speed too fast / assuming that the road straightens-out after the VP / failure to use the correct Course or use the front brake anywhere.

All of these riders are approaching at the same Entry Speed and are on the same original Course. Please also remember that there is very big hill on the left-hand side which offers limited Forward / Left Visibility. Oh, and don't forget the sheer drop on the right-hand side of the road.

Or, you can do it properly!

If you were out in the open countryside and are riding along with massive amounts of all-round visibility then you could use the entire width of the road, rather than just the width of the lane. Obviously, you would need to know that there are no hidden turns, lay-bys or dips in the road (etc) waiting to catch you out. Here's another diagram to show the manoeuvre :-

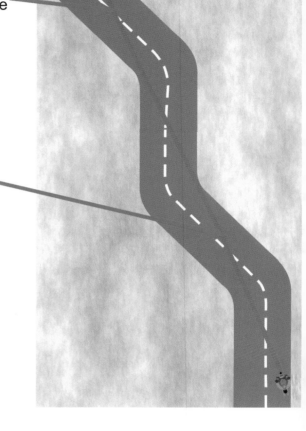

As you can see, the green line shows a very smooth Course through all 4 bends. You can also see that the bike would be almost upright throughout, meaning that there are plenty of places to straighten the bike up and brake, if necessary.

If you look closely, you will see that the rider actually takes the set of bends by banking only once to the left and once to the right.

As you can see, because of the excellent forward visibility, a wide, flowing Course can be used, rather than a more restricted line. This Course means that you and the bike have less work to do.

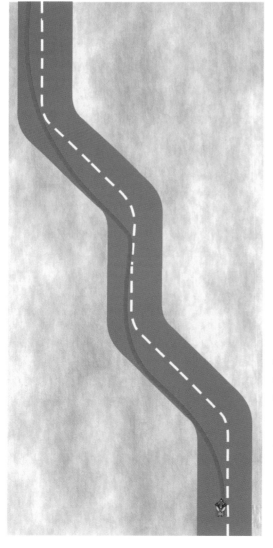

Here's the rider on the same road executing a Course using only the left-hand lane. Because the rider here is treating all 4 bends as separate items, the speed will have to be lower, and the rider and bike will be working so much harder.

Obviously, this is the Course to use if there is on-coming traffic or when your forward visibility is restricted.

So, to close this chapter, let's look at some more real-life examples :-

A simple right-hand band over a bridge ?

Look again. Did you spot the road-signs ?
(Yes ! There's 2 !)

Now do you see the junction up ahead on the left ?

Mobile library, junction to your left, and another up-ahead, with a van about to overtake the parked car - or is it turning right ?

Be ready fo pedestrians stepping out from behind the library.

Keeping to the right of the lane will give you the best angle of visibility whilst avoiding the blind junction to your left.

Don't just look at what's directly in front of you. Yes, the junction to your left is clear, but did you see where the road goes ?

How many things are there to take into consideration in this next example ? OK, so there's 'SLOW' painted on the road, a 'Reduce Speed Now' sign and a 'Road Narrows' sign. What about the car up ahead on the right ? Is it going to pull out ?

Did you spot th 4x4 and the white van coming towards you, just where the road narrows ?

The trees overhang the road, the tarmac will be shaded, meaning that the road surface might be damp.

The road makings also tell you that there's a solid white line coming-up as you enter a right-hand bend.

Is anything going to overtake you before you get there ?

Although you can't see it, there's a junction to your left coming-up. The give-away is the sign on your right and the 'dixie' mirror'. This would suggest that it's a 'blind bend', so you can take a wide Course (as shown).

Hands-up if you spotted the 'left bend' sign.

It's a lovely country road on a sunny day and you can see that the road bends round to the left. The sea looks great.

Did you notice the sheep at the side of the road ? Are there any more, just around the bend ?

It's easy to spot the fact that the road here has a dip, but did you notice that there is a small kink to the left ? This could easily throw you off-course.

Did you spot the farm entrance to the right ?

The green Course / Line through this bend gives you the maximum amount of visibility. The red line shows how little forward visibility you would have taking a bad line. You never know what's around the next bend.

The road markings disappear half-way through the bend because the road simply isn't wide enough. This wouldn't be a problem on a clear road like this, but what if a car towing a caravan was there ? Or a bus ? Or a truck ?

Bonus points for spotting the left-turn sign.

Chapter 7 - Looking after your machine and you

Your bike

This section deals with looking after your bike, the important stuff, and what considerations you need to take into account for some of it's components. A motorcycle is, at the end of the day, a machine and all machines need maintaining from time to time and some components might even need replacing. Let's start with tyres.

Tyres are one of the most important components fitted to a motorcycle and must be treated as such and it's worth bearing in mind that on a modern, large-capacity superbike, there is about the same contact area as the palm of your hand. That's both tyres added together ! That's how important it is to fit your bike with good quality tyres. Smaller capacity machines will, usually, be fitted with thinner tyres which won't have as much surface contact.

A brand-new tyre will still have remnants of it's releasing agent, which is used as part of the manufacturing process. Obviously, the job of a releasing agent is to ensure that the tyre didn't stick to the mould during the manufacturing process, but it will retain that same functionality when in contact with the road surface. In other words, it won't stick very well until the releasing agent has been gently worn away with careful use during a 'running-in' period.

The legal minimum tread depth for a motorcycle tyre is only 1mm, which is nothing when you think how deep (maybe 2mm) rainwater is during a sudden shower or downpour. With less tread available to disperse the water, there is a significantly higher risk of you 'aqua-planing' - which is where your tyre (or tyres) lose contact with the road and 'skim' on top of the layer of water.

Under-inflated tyres will lose some, or all, of their rain-displacing qualities as the treads will be forced to close-up. That situation can lead to the tyre having no tread and will, effectively, behave like a slick tyre which, in the wet, is going to be very dangerous. Cornering with an under-inflated tyre can cause the tyre to detach itself from the wheel rim with, often lethal, results. An over-inflated tyre will provide less of a footprint, a contact patch, on the road than one which is correctly inflated so braking, as well as accelerating, would be severely affected.

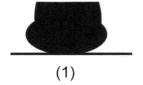
(1)

(2)

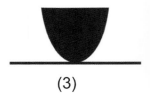
(3)

This illustration represents an under-inflated tyre (1), an over-inflated tyre (2) and a tyre at the correct pressure (3). Tyre manufacturers go to enormous lengths to ensure that their tyres perform as well as they can under most conditions, but only if the tyre is at the correct pressure, so only check your tyre pressures when the tyres are cold in order to get an accurate reading.

Don't forget that when the bike is banked over, there is more tyre contact area due to centrifugal force and friction also comes into play, which helps to give you better grip, and is the reason why you should make sure that your tyres are at the correct pressure.

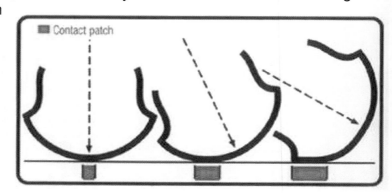

If you want more info about tyres, may I suggest you take a look at :-
Http://max.xbhp.com/all-about-tyres/tyre-science/#.V5kJ2KIii6g

Chains are the most usual way of transmitting the engine's power to the back wheel. Some bikes are fitted with shaft-drive and some even use a reinforced 'rubber' belt but generally, they're chain-driven. The chain is made of links, with rubber seals on the rivets between the outer plate and the inner roller which help to keep crud, salt and water from the steel rollers.

If the rollers get rusty through neglect, they will, in turn, destroy the chain, usually taking the front and rear sprockets with them. On a regular basis, depending on what mileage you ride and what the weather's like, keep a close eye on your rear chain and lubricate it accordingly. Remember, chains have 4 sides, not just the one that you always see. Lubricate the entire chain - front / back / top / bottom. At the same time, make sure that the chain's tension is as per your bike's manual.

A chain that is too loose is likely to come off the sprockets, potentially locking the back wheel solid. A chain that is too tight is very likely to snap and if it did, it could easily slice straight through your ankle - with or without bike boots on !

If, whilst riding along, you notice that your chain has become 'noisy' in a certain part of it's revolution, then it will usually be because the chain has developed what is called a 'tight-spot'. In English, it's because a few links have become rusty inside the rollers and the only cure is a new chain.

Whenever you're changing the chain, it's alway a good idea to check both of the sprockets aswell and replace them if the teeth look 'hooked'.

Brake Pads are there to stop you and the bike and there has been a lot of development over the years in brake pad technology. The two types are referred to as 'organic' and 'sintered'. Sintered pads contain copper, are Standard Equipment on 99% of all motorcycles and are the most powerful

version of brake pads. If the pads wear out, you'll be wearing-away your brake disk(s) every time you brake. If nothing else, the horrendous squeal should give you a clue (mechanics refer to it as 'metal on metal' because there's no brake lining left.) The picture here's an example of a sintered brake pad.

Engine Oil is, basically, the blood of your bike's engine so always replace it in line with your manufacturer's recommendations and always use a good quality oil. Engine Oil comes in 3 versions - Conventional (Organic), Semi-Synthetic and Fully Synthetic with Fully Synthetic being the most commonly used today. Make sure that you replace you oil with the correct SAE (Viscosity) rating (refer to your Owner's manual) as different types of engines sometimes require a different range. SAE 5/10, for example, would not be suitable in a Japanese motorcycle engine which usually uses SAE 10/40. If you're not sure, take your bike to a reputable motorcycle mechanic. Whenever you change the engine oil, it's vital that you also change the oil filter. The job of the oil filter is to trap and keep all of the Particular Matter that's in your engine oil. As such, the oil filter is one of the most vital, and sometimes neglected, components inside your engine which also helps lower the degradation damage done to engine oil by oxidation. Again, if you're not sure, take your bike to a reputable motorcycle mechanic.

Mechanical Sympathy is something which you should have with your bike's engine. Warm the engine up first, before you start your journey, so that the engine's oil gets to it's working temperature. Remember that during the first few seconds of starting an engine, the oil has to get into every bearing, nook and crevice before it will able to protect your engine properly, so don't go firing it up from cold and cracking the throttle wide open. Remember, that's the engine that you might need to rely on one day.

Storing your bike over winter.

If you decide to take your bike off the road for those horrible winter months, then there's a couple of things that you need to know.

Firstly, you can SORN (Statutory Off Road Notification) your vehicle and reclaim any unused 'road tax'. If you pay your road tax monthly, then the Standing Order will be cancelled from the end of that month.

Secondly, as long as your bike isn't being stored either on the road or in a 'public place', you can cancel your Insurance. If the bike isn't on private land, you could get a fixed penalty of £100. have your vehicle wheel-clamped, impounded or destroyed and face a court prosecution, with a possible maximum fine of £1,000. (Source :- https://www.gov.uk/make-a-sorn)

If you can, store your bike on paddock-stands - this will stop the tyres developing a 'flat-spot' over the winter. If not, then make sure that you move the bike periodically so that it's not always parked on the same part of the tyre.

If you're bike's being stored outside (in your garden, for example), then make sure that you're bike's drive-chain (if it has one) is well oiled and that you cover your brake disks / calipers with something like a bin bag taped-up. This will help stop the disks / brakes from going rusty and seizing.

Finally, disconnect the bike's battery or remove the master fuse. This will stop the battery being slowly drained by your bike's fuel gauge over the winter. If your bike has an alarm, then there are products such as a 'battery optimizer' or a trickle-charger available.

Motorcycle Ergonomics

Your physical build may limit the type of bike that you can ride. For example, if you're of small stature, then a massively-tall Adventure bike might be out of your reach, so to speak. Even a Chopper or Cruiser, which have a low seat-height, might be fitted with 'Ape-hanger' handlebars. This set of pictures show a small selection of the various styles readily-available.

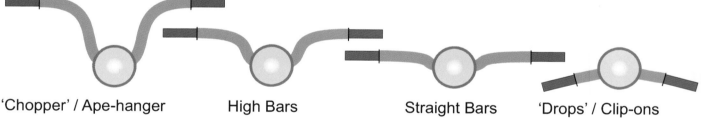

'Chopper' / Ape-hanger　　　　High Bars　　　　Straight Bars　　　'Drops' / Clip-ons

Some bikes have Universal Handlebar clamps, meaning that you can change them to your heart's content but if you're fitting really high handlebars to a bike with standard Straight bars, then you'll need to lengthen the wiring harness, front brake and clutch pipes / cables. Other bike models may be fitted with cast-aluminium handlebars and can't be changed.

If you're of massive stature, then you're going to struggle riding a small-capacity motorcycle, scooter or moped. I pity the poor piston that has to propel that much bulk. 'Race-Replica' motorcycles may also pose a problem, due to their compact size.

Once you've decided on the style of bike you want, you need to spend a bit of time making the bike fit you. Making sure that you can see what's behind you is vital, so adjust the mirrors first. On most bikes, you can adjust the angle of the handlebars, both of the front levers, both sets of switchgear, the rear bake pedal as well as the position of the gear lever, can all be customised to your particular preferences. If you're buying second-hand, the previous owner could have set the bike up to their build / preferences, which might be the total opposite to yours. With regards to the clutch and brake levers, there are numerous after-market replacements which are as good as, or better, than the factory-fitted items. Some offer adjustable lever positions for people who might have a shorter span, or just prefer the lever being closer to the handlebars.

Legal Paperwork

Driving Licence - This serves as your proof of being entitled to ride your bike on the road. If you're a Learner, you CANNOT take a pillion UNLESS that pillion holds a valid, full, UK motorcycle licence. If you have a full car and motorcycle licence, remember that any Penalty Points that you may be given all go on the same Licence - they're not different Licences, merely different entitlements.

Insurance can be very expensive, particularly for the young or inexperienced, but NOT having it can prove even more expensive if you get caught and prosecuted for not being insured. In the eyes of the law, it's almost as bad as drink-driving. The Offence stays on your Licence for 4 years, with the subsequent 'x00% loading' on every insurance quote that you'll get, car or bike. Always tell the truth when applying for insurance, otherwise you may find yourself being subject to an investigation during a claim which may leave you with conditions being imposed on your insurance. Once again, this will put another 'x00% loading' on any future insurance quote.

If you own a motorcycle, it MUST be insured, otherwise you'll receive an automatic fine through the post ! Contact a reputable motorcycle Insurance Broker if you have any concerns.

M.O.T. (Ministry Of Transport) Certificate is required on every motorcycle over 3 years old, from date of Original Registration. It's basically a safety and road-worthyness check and covers the frame, wheels, brakes, brake-lines, tyres, chain/ sprockets, shock absorber(s), front forks, headlight, brake lights, horn, indicators and exhaust. Just because a bike has an MOT Certificate, it does NOT guarantee a vehicle's road-worthyness 6 months down the line. In fact, a few cynics would say that an MOT Certificate is only 'valid' on the day it was issued ... In some cases, a motorcycle without a valid MOT Certificate being used on the roads would not be insured as there is usually a clause in your Insurance Policy which would read along the lines of 'providing that the vehicle has a valid MOT Certificate, where applicable'. No MOT ? No insurance !!

V5 Registration Document is a legal document, otherwise known as a 'log-book', which gives details of the vehicle such as registration number, frame and engine numbers, engine size and seating capacity. It also shows when the vehicle was first new, together with how many previous keepers the bike's had. 'Learner bikes' will, generally, have had more previous keepers than bigger bikes as they're not the sort of bike you keep for very long after you've passed your test. Don't let a high number of former keepers put you off a 125, just think about how long you plan to keep it for.

Remember, the registered keeper is not, necessarily, the legal owner. On the front page it reads "This document is not proof of ownership", so if you're buying privately, be aware of this fact.

Whenever you buy or sell a bike, always get the V5 changed over to your name as quickly as possible to much sure that you won't be having an unwanted chat with the local constabulary about something that you didn't do or know anything about.

If you're buying privately, always make sure that the V5 details match the bike and that you're dealing with the registered keeper, if possible, at the address on the V5. Take a (preferably mechanically-minded) mate with you so that you've got a witness to everything said and done.

In case of an accident you'll need to know your rights and legal responsibilities. If you unlucky enough to be in an accident, you MUST stop and give your name, address and Vehicle Registration Number to anybody with 'reasonable grounds' for such information. This applies whether the accident was your fault or not. Full a fuller breakdown, please visit :- https://www.askthe.police.uk/content/Q894.htm. where there's a wealth of information on the subject.

If you're in any doubt as to an insurance claim, refer to the matter to an specialist Solicitor, preferably one who knows the difference between a Bungee Cord and a Belly Pan. You do NOT have to use the one provided by your Insurance Company, but get a few quotes first as rates vary.

Vehicle Security is something which you should take seriously because thieves can strike at any time. A smaller-capacity bike (especially the off-road type) is easy to throw in the back of a van so always try and chain your bike to something which can't be moved, such as a lamp-post, for example. Larger-capacity bikes aren't exempt either, especially if your bike's very 'desirable' or much sought-after among the criminal fraternity. When a bike is targeted, a team of 4 blokes put a scaffold pole through each wheel, pick it up and throw it in the back of a refrigerated lorry, as the insulation deadens the sound of any alarm going-off.

Whenever you park your bike up, get into the habit of always using the bike's steering lock but that should never replace additional security such as a disk-lock or a padlock and chain.

Disk-locks, like the example shown here are small, cheap (from about £25), easy to carry and a very good deterrent for the opportune thief.

However, they can only stop the bike from being rolled forwards or backwards a won't stop the bike from being carried-away.

A padlock and chain, like the one shown here, are made using forged, hardened steel and cost less than £100 - which is probably cheaper than your insurance Excess is ...

If you do choose to use a padlock and chain, carry it on the bike using a bungee cord rather than have it sloped over your shoulder, across you body. The reason for that is very simple :- imagine what would happen if you were knocked off your bike and landed on your back from 3 ft up with thick chain-links running across your spine ....

You may want to use a padlock and chain in conjunction with some sort of ground anchor, making it very difficult for thieves to deprive you of your pride and joy. Prices range from (Just over) £20-£150+.

If you rent your house / lock-up, make sure that you get the landlord's permission before you go drilling massive holes in the concrete !

Clothing

A picture, as the saying goes, paints a thousand words, so here's three thousand words :-

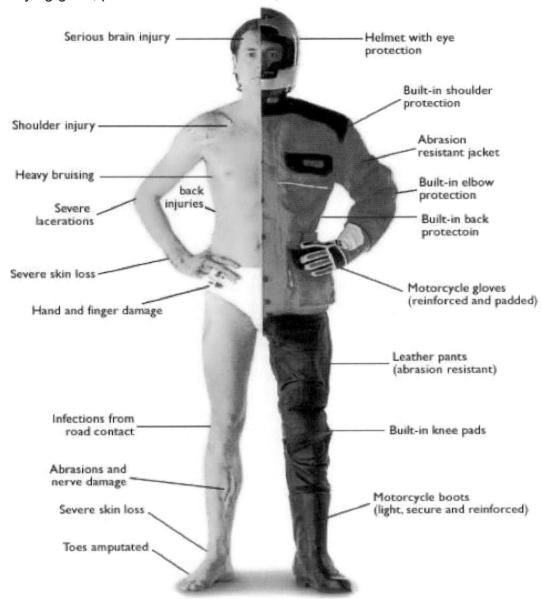

- Serious brain injury
- Helmet with eye protection
- Built-in shoulder protection
- Shoulder injury
- Abrasion resistant jacket
- Heavy bruising
- back injuries
- Built-in elbow protection
- Severe lacerations
- Built-in back protectoin
- Severe skin loss
- Hand and finger damage
- Motorcycle gloves (reinforced and padded)
- Leather pants (abrasion resistant)
- Infections from road contact
- Built-in knee pads
- Abrasions and nerve damage
- Severe skin loss
- Motorcycle boots (light, secure and reinforced)
- Toes amputated

Think about these pictures before you go jumping onto your bike wearing flip-flops and a pair of shorts and a tee-shirt, just because the sun happens to be shining for a couple of hours.

Would you rather sweat or bleed? Put safety first. ALWAYS WEAR PROPER RIDING GEAR

DRESS FOR THE SLIDE NOT THE RIDE

Clothing

Your clothing is the only thing between you and the surface of the road if you should be unfortunate enough to come off your bike. The abrasive properties of the road's surface should never be underestimated. Cast your mind back to when you were running as a youngster and fell over. What was the first thing to hit the ground ? The human brain is hard-wired to protect itself at all times and will try to put your hands and arms out in order to protect your head. As the saying goes 'no matter what the weather, always wear the leather' as it is a lightweight, extremely abrasive-resistant material.

Advances in modern materials such as Kevlar and Carbon Fibre have meant that clothing - both leather and textile - have been enhanced with added protection in the shape of built-in spine protectors and the like. Jackets, trousers, boots and gloves have all benefited from new technologies but you will have to expect to pay a little bit more. Always buy the highest quality that you can afford as buying cheap is a false economy where motorcycle clothing is concerned. Leather jeans or a jacket that cost around £200 (new) will probably outlast you. If you're not able to afford new kit, on-line auctions are a great place to snap-up unwanted motorcycle clothing or try your local Army & Navy store.

Buy clothing that is appropriate to your bike usage – if you're commuting 50 miles per day, in all weathers – then buy gear that would be up to the job. If you are wearing laced-up boots on a motorcycle, always remember to tuck all of the laces into your boots on the side which will be further from the motorcycle. Doing this will prevent the laces becoming entangled on the front footrest, stopping your foot in mid-air as you try to put your foot down and making you look a fool at a set of traffic lights.

Gloves

Imagine if your boss (for example) told you to put the palm of your hand against a rapidly-spinning sanding disk, you'd want to be wearing 'suitable protection', so why would you ever **not** wear gloves on a motorbike ? The skin on the palm of your hand is only about 1.5 mm thick, at best. After that you're grinding muscle, ligaments, veins and then bones away. I wonder how long it would be before you would master as simple a task as wiping your own backside with a surgically-implanted hook ? Think about that before you ride off without wearing gloves !

If you are going to be riding your bike in all weathers it is strongly advised for you to wear leather gloves which have been manufactured using waterproof components such as Gortex or similar. It is difficult to concentrate with cold, wet hands and instead of focusing on your surroundings, looking for and identifying hazards, you'll be agonising over your freezing-cold, wet fingers. Care must be taken not to warm your hands up too quickly afterwards as this could lead to chilblains, which can become itchy, swollen and painful for about a week. Wet gloves will seriously increase the amount of wind-chill factor, reducing the temperatures experienced even more. Clothing which may prove to be suitable during the warmer summer months may prove to be insufficient during the colder winter months and most people who ride all year round will have separate, heavier-duty clothing for winter use.

Under-Layers

As the old saying goes, lots of thinner under-layers will keep you warmer than one larger one. In cold weather, wear thermal underclothes or buy electrically-heated clothing, including gloves, which run off the bike's battery.

Helmet

Your helmet is another vital piece of kit and should be looked-after and replaced in accordance with the manufacturer's guidelines. All helmets have to pass an EU Standard but a cheap helmet will probably not be as comfortable, or as well finished, as an expensive helmet. It might let rain in through an air-vent or the visor won't seal properly after a couple of weeks, meaning that the visor might 'whistle' at certain speeds. As with most things in life, comfort comes at a price so, if you can afford it, buy a good quality helmet, make sure that it fits you properly and take care of it. Whether you buy a cheap, polycarbonate open-face helmet, or the very latest full-face composite model, the protective layer inside is still made of the same stuff - polystyrene. This is why you should never put your helmet base-down over your bike's petrol filler-cap, especially on a hot day, as the petrol vapours will attack and destroy the polystyrene lining of your helmet. Try to avoid putting your helmet in such a position that it will fall or get damaged.

Visor

A scratch or a dent in your visor can seriously impair your vision especially in the wet, bright sunlight or at night where there are streetlights or vehicle headlights. A scratch is even worse if it's in a focal spot so always replace your visor it if it gets damaged. A new visor is cheaper to replace than your bike is ..

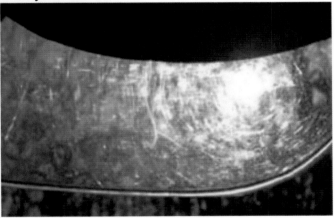

The view out of a badly scratched visor on a sunny day

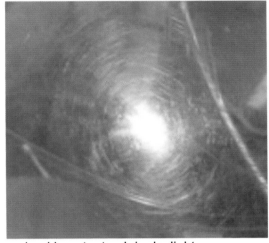

Looking at a torch in daylight

Being prepared for wet weather

Your visor and glasses, if worn, will become misted-up in rain or cold temperatures so always carry a readily-available cleaning cloth, or plenty of dry tissue, in a waterproof bag. Also use a plastic, waterproof bag to carry your mobile phone in, and any other sensitive electrical device, when riding in wet conditions.

Riding at night in wet weather is hard enough without having a blurry spot to try and see through or around. Always keep your visor clean, inside and out and if you need to clean your visor whilst you're out riding, those little hand-wipes that you get from certain fast-food outlets are also very good at cleaning crud off visors. Riding in the direction of the sun, especially in winter, can cause damage to your vision and a cheap, effective way to block out the sun is to use insulation tape on the <u>inside</u> of your visor to cover the area between the top of the visor and the top of your normal field of vision.

Weather-watching

Keeping a casual eye on the skies above might help you avoid being suddenly caught-out by a rain-shower. In this picture, the clouds were blowing over from left to right and you can see the rain already falling on the far left of the picture. The air will usually become cooler and, with practice, you will be able to smell an imminent shower.

Time to find somewhere safe to park-up and stick the water-proofs on and make sure that your electrical devices are safely stashed !

A downpour after a long dry spell will make the roads almost as slippery as ice does. This is due to the fact that, in hot weather, the road-surface expands and the pores in the road's surface collect bit of oil, bits of diesel and tiny fragments of tyre rubber. As the rain cools the surface of the road, it causes it to contract and squeezes all of the road-bourne gunk onto the road-surface of the road, under the layer of water. (Think acne-ridden teenager's face with all of the zits exploding at once !) Your tyres are on top of that layer of water, and we all know what happens when you mix oil and water !

The easiest way to detect the conditions described above is to smell the air. Hot tarmac and cold rain creates a particularly recognisable aroma in the air. The road-surface will be greasy so you should ride accordingly.

When you upgrade to a larger-capacity or higher-performance motorbike take the time to fully get used to it. Bigger bikes require heavier frames, bigger brakes, wider tyres, heavier wheels, more substantial forks and many, many other components add more weight than what you might be used to.

Accelerating, braking, turning, cornering - and all aspects of the machine's handling - will need to be re-mastered by you, and will happen as you get used to the changes. Practice and experience will give you knowledge. Remember the formula :- High self-belief x limited skill = high crash / injury probability.

The type of bike that you ride should suit your style of riding and what you want to do during your motorcycle career. It's no good buying a 'cruiser' if you prefer ripping-up a few bends at the weekend, or choosing a middle-weight sports machine if you want to go camping for a fortnight with a pillion, or 'green-laning' on a sports bike. I'm sure you get the idea ...

With that in mind, I've drawn-up a guidance table to show the differences between different styles of motorbikes, the different power that they produce, the differing dry weight and speed (where possible) :-

Make / Model	Max power HP / Kw	Max Torque Nm / Kgm	Dry Weight KG / LBS	Max Speed KPH / MPH
Honda CB 125	13.6 / 10 @10,000 rpm	10.6 / 1.08	127 / 280 1	12.7 / 70.02
CBR 600RR	118 / 88.1 @13,500 rpm	66 / 6.79	186 / 410	255.3 /158.6
BMW 1200GS	98 / 73 @10,000 rpm	115 / 11.7	225 / 496	193 /120
Harley Davidson Electra Glide (1,584 cc)	(no info available)	124.7 / 12.7	386 / 850	(no info available)
Ducati 1200 Multistrada	160 / 117.7 @ 9,500 rpm	136 / 13.9	208 / 458	(no info available)
Kawasaki ZZR1400	187 / 139.45 @ 9,500 rpm	126 / 13.87	264 / 584	295.6 /188.7
(source - http://www.motorcyclespecs.co.za - July 2016)				E&OE

Honda CB 125

Honda CBR600RR

BMW 1200GS

Harley Davidson Electra Glide

Ducati 1200 Multistrada

Kawasaki ZZR1400

This is only a small fraction of the variety of types motorcycles available, and it's only meant as an introduction to what's out there. Choose a bike that will suit your intended purposes .... 'Horses for Courses' as the saying goes.

Chapter Eight - BikerCraft

BikerCraft

This chapter is a mixture of real-world experience, advice, learned wisdom and - in places - just plain-old common sense.

Ensure that you always concentrate on what is up ahead, all around you, as well as behind you. **Observation / Concentration - Riding Rule #1.** I've been deliberately repeating that phrase throughout the book, just to give you some idea about how much concentration is needed - at ALL times ! Keep an eye on what is going-on all around you, then use that full observation, and your experience, to pro-actively try to prepare for what lies up-ahead. Plan your course, plan your position and identify any and all potential hazards then take whatever action you deem necessary to make things a little safer for yourself.

Always try to leave plenty of space between you and the vehicle in front of you. Everybody has to learn thinking distances, braking distances and overall stopping distances as part of their test but who can actually, realistically or accurately measure something seventy five feet away whilst travelling at thirty miles per hour ? The '2-Second Rule', which was described back in Chapter Three, is very useful to help you gauge a <u>minimum</u> safe distance, but the Rule becomes flawed at higher speeds and you must also bear in mind that the Rule assumes things like an alert, observant rider, good road conditions, good road surface, good tyres, good brakes and a well-controlled stop etc.

The Highway Code's calculation for Overall Stopping Distances was first derived in 1946 with drivers being placed in a simulator and being asked to press a pedal every time that they saw a light bulb come on. That's how they (incorrectly) came-up with a Reaction Time of just 0.7 seconds. Obviously, in the real world, that would be utterly unrealistic, as you would have to be riding everywhere, continually expecting to have to do an Emergency Stop at any point, every inch of the way. You'd be a nervous wreck !

To show you how the Rule breaks, let's assume you're extremely focussed, fully alert and following a vehicle, with a 2 second gap back to you, which suddenly, and completely, stops.

Let's begin at 30 MPH -

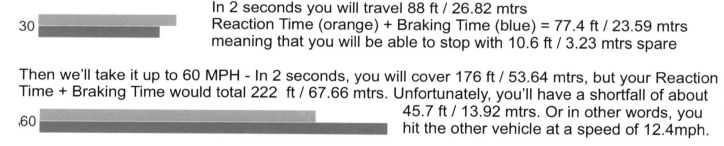

In 2 seconds you will travel 88 ft / 26.82 mtrs
Reaction Time (orange) + Braking Time (blue) = 77.4 ft / 23.59 mtrs
meaning that you will be able to stop with 10.6 ft / 3.23 mtrs spare

Then we'll take it up to 60 MPH - In 2 seconds, you will cover 176 ft / 53.64 mtrs, but your Reaction Time + Braking Time would total 222 ft / 67.66 mtrs. Unfortunately, you'll have a shortfall of about 45.7 ft / 13.92 mtrs. Or in other words, you hit the other vehicle at a speed of 12.4mph.

But look what happens when we take it up to 90 MPH, which is not uncommon on most of Britain's motorways these days. This time, 2 seconds = 264 ft / 80.46 mtrs. Your Reaction Time, added to your Braking Time, would total 367 ft / 111.86 mtrs, meaning that, once gain, you will have a shortfall, except that the shortfall will be about 169 ft / 51.51 mtrs. The impact speed, however, will be 35.1 MPH.

As I said at the beginning, the diagrams above are based on a Reaction Time of 1 second, which would not be unreasonable, so long as the rider was fresh, totally alert, in a 'best case' scenario, with good all-round visibility and very few hazards to contend with.

You might think that with improved tyre technology, advance braking systems (including Anti-lock Brakes), race-developed suspension and modern road construction materials, that Overall Stopping Distances would be getting shorter. However, that is not the case. Due to, what are called, 'increased levels of distraction' and 'lifestyle choices', Her Majesty's Courts now base their calculations on a Reaction Time of 1.5 seconds. That figure has been proven by Police Accident Investigators as evidence in Case Law. Let's just think about that for a second ...... 'Increased levels of distraction' means that there are so many gadgets and warning lights in today's modern cars, that drivers allow themselves to be distracted. Electrically heated leather seats with double arm-rests, climate control, Bluetooth, Sat-Nav, 20-speaker DAB Ghetto-blaster and Talking Text Systems are pretty-much standard equipment these days. 'Lifestyle choices' might suggest that people are becoming more sloth-like when they're driving, or becoming more apathetic or lackadaisical. Or maybe it's because their vehicle has multi award-winning impact and safety features ? Effectively, car manufacturers have done their bit to wipe-out 50 years of Research and Development ! But what does that mean to us motorcyclists ? Let's see how that figure of 1.5 seconds Reaction Time looks when we compare it to the Highway Code's Overall Stopping Distances graph :-

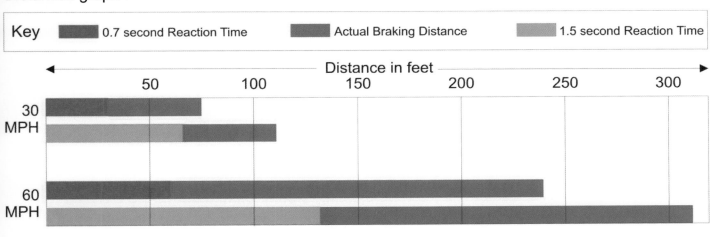

So, really, at anything under 50 MPH, 2 seconds is probably OK for you to use as a _bare minimum,_ but at anything over that, perhaps you should add another second. In wet conditions, double your gap, as you can't brake as hard in the wet on a motorbike. I suggest that you remember this Rule as the 'x Second Rule', with 'x' being 2, 3, 4 or 6 seconds, instead of the '2 second Rule', in order that you don't always default to using 2 seconds. This is especially important if you're riding on differing roads with different speeds and traffic etc.

With modern driving conditions, particularly on motorways, and today's ever-conjested roads, you should learn to _expect_ a vehicle to move into your 'x second space', so you will then need to readjust to the new distance accordingly. Insurance companies always take the view that if you run into the back of another vehicle, then it's automatically your fault.

A good rider will always be in a position of maximum control, fully aware of the surrounding environment and conditions. Maximum control means knowing your own limits, the machine's limits, and riding just below them. Never try to exceed your own limits, or take them for granted and don't ever push a bike, or the bike's tyres, past their limitations. Integration of BikerCraft's System into your everyday riding will not only provide you with a methodical process by which you can ascertain any visible threat, have your action already planned and in execution. That's the sign of a competent, skillful rider. The bike doesn't ever, ever make the rider, regardless of how expensive or how exotic the bike in question might be. I hope that by reading this book, you will become a better, competent and more confident rider that has the ability to go wherever the feeling takes you.

A swan can seem elegant and graceful as it stays in the same spot on a river, but underneath the water, It's paddling-away like crazy, just to stay in the same spot. It's the same for an experienced, road-hardened rider. It might look like the rider is just gliding along, but in the rider's head is a constant plasma-storm of decisions going-on. Both look elegant to the observer though, if you get it right.

One thing which is frequently overlooked, where riding motorcycles is concerned, is something referred to as 'wind-chill'. If you were stood in the middle of a field, with a 30 MPH wind blowing at you, you would expect your temperature to be lowered by the wind. Well, it's exactly the same effect if you are travelling at 30 MPH and there is no other wind. On a very hot day, it's nice to feel the cooling breeze wafting through your clothing but things can turn pretty nasty once the temperature starts to plummet. Even though wind-chill is more of an issue during the colder winter months, you might find that what starts-out as a bright sunny day can often end-up turning chilly as the day wears on. Altitude can also have an effect, as the temperature will drop between 1-3 degrees (C) for every 1,000 feet of elevation. If you plan going out for a ride on a reasonably warm, sunny afternoon for a few hours, be prepared for colder temperatures later-on when you'll be riding your bike back home, particularly if the sun has set. Bungee a sweatshirt to your pillion seat (for example) or tie it around your waist - you'll be glad of it when the temperature drops !

As an example, at 30 mph, in a cool-feeling 15° C, it will feel more like 12° C on the bike but with an ambient air temperature of a lowly 5° C, at the same speed, it will feel more like just below -1° on any forward-facing exposed patches of skin such as your nose or under your chin. This graph gives a visual overview for a speed of 30MPH and clearly demonstrates the difference that air temperature makes.

The ambient (air) temperature range is 15° different but the wind-chill is over 20° different ! At 70 MPH, with an ambient temperature of 15° C, your wind-chill factor would be just below 11° C but bear in mind that an ambient air temperature of 10°C, at that speed, would put your wind-chill factor at somewhere just below 4°. If it was around freezing point and you were riding at 70 MPH, then the wind-chill factor would drop down to a hypothermia-inducing -11° C and your reaction times will be far longer and you won't feel as much feed-back from the bike. If your core body (your torso) temperature drops by only 2° C from it's normal 37° C, you're extremely likely to feel the on-set of hypothermia. Hypothermia kills ! Riding for any prolonged period of time with a low wind-chill temperature can cause the muscles in your hands, neck, legs and feet to cramp-up which is not only excruciatingly painful, but extremely dangerous as you will not be able to concentrate on what's going-on around you. Cold muscles will react much, much slower than warm ones and your fingers will be numb with cold. Concentrating on riding would be severely difficult as the only thing that will be on your mind will be the agonising cold. If you find yourself in that position, find somewhere like a petrol station or shop where you could warm your hands and feet up. If not, simply walking around and moving your arms around will generate heat but it is best done whilst keeping your motorcycling clothing on as you will be able to generate a layer of warm air between your clothing and your skin. Especially keep your helmet on as most body heat, as every school-kid knows, is lost through the head. Take this time to make sure that any air-vents on your helmet or clothing are closed, otherwise vital heat will be lost as you ride along. This picture is a representation of a thermal imaging camera image and shows how heat is lost.

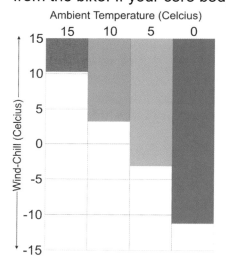

Notice how the torso shows red, then orange (warm), then goes through to green (cold) to blue (ice cold) in the arms and through the neck and head. The further that the blood has to flow, your arms and legs for example, the cooler it becomes. Hypothermia sets-in when the torso would show as green or blue.

Filtering, Whilst completely legal (Highway Code Rule 88), it can be considered to be extremely dangerous due to the close proximity of other vehicles on either side of you. There is no real room for escape so always ensure that are ready to stop your machine in a very short distance and the technique to that is to keep your speed down. Whilst filtering between two lines of stationary or slow-moving traffic during day-light hours, switch your headlight to main-beam to act as a visual warning. Filtering between two rows of cars going in the same direction is just as dangerous as

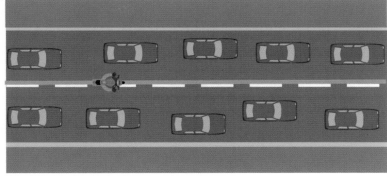

riding between two rows of cars going in the opposite direction. Don't assume that traffic coming towards you will be inclined, or able, to move out of your way. Also, don't forget that traffic moving towards you will be reducing the amount of room, therefore time, between your motorcycle and their vehicle. You'll also have to keep an eye out for pedestrians randomly running-out between other vehicles. To reiterate once again, filtering on a motorcycle is perfectly legal but in the event of an accident, the motorcyclist is usually blamed (rightly or wrongly).

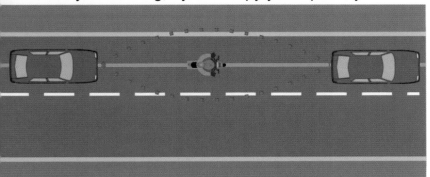

Whenever you're riding, try to occupy your space, your 'bubble', defensively and make use of different positions to give you differing views. Always pay attention and concentrate on what is going -on all around you and react accordingly.
Riding Rule #1.

Riding with a pillion can greatly increase the weight of the bike and that extra weight must be taken into account when accelerating, braking and cornering. Make sure that you adjust the bike's front and rear suspension first, according to your owner's handbook for your bike and increase the tyre pressures in line with the tyre manufacturer's instructions.

There's a couple of rules from the Highway Code which you must know about before taking a pillion, so I've included them here :- Rule #85 states 'You MUST NOT carry more than one pillion passenger who MUST sit astride the machine on a proper seat. They should face forward with both feet on the footrests.' Whilst Rule #83 clarifies that 'both the rider and pillion must wear an approved helmet, which must fit properly and be fastened correctly. The visors should be free from scratches and be clean.'

Take time to fully familiarise (educate) the pillion with the bike. It might sound daft but you should explain how they should even get on and off the bike if they've never done it before. The normal way is for you to be sat on the motorcycle, with both of your feet firmly on the ground, with your legs straight, holding the Handlebars with the front brake lever pulled-in.

Next, your pillion should place their left foot on the rear left footrest ....

.... with their left hand on your left shoulder ....

.... with their right hand placed either on the seat, rack or rear bodywork of the bike.

By straightening their left leg and by using their left arm, they will then be able to sling their right leg over the bike and onto the right rear footrest and get themself comfortable. As the pillion mounts the bike, all of their weight will be directed through your left leg and left shoulder, so be ready for the extra strain. Getting off the bike is a reversal of the same process. Obviously, always make sure that you've got both of your feet firmly on the ground, and that the front brake is fully on whenever your pillion gets on or off the bike.

Your pillion will also need to know how to sit during normal riding and my advice to pillions is for them to sit as if they were a sack of potatoes and hold-on the rear grab-rail or rack . It's your responsibility to ensure that the pillion is holding-on securely at all times and you should make it clear to them that under acceleration, their mass will also be subject to Weight-Transference and that if they're not holding on properly, their feet can easily rise off the footrests (due to 'Angular Momentum') and that their body will probably be tipped backwards over the rear of the motorcycle. Make allowances for the extra weight during acceleration, particularly when you're planning an overtaking manoeuvre. Take the time to allow your pillion to adapt to your riding style and for them to grow their confidence and trust in your abilities.

A smooth gear change will become more important when a pillion is carried unless, that is, you like to hear and feel the back of your helmet being bumped by the pillion's helmet every time you change gear ! Never try to impress a pillion with how fast your bike can go, and remember that you will need to allow extra braking distance due to the increased load. Remember what happens when you double your speed ? Well the distances get even bigger when you add more weight to the motorcycle. Always bear in mind that, in the event of an accident, the pillion usually comes off worst.

You'll also need to educate your pillion about what happens to the bike during braking because, unlike a car, a pillion becomes an intrinsic, integral part of the whole package. Take the time to explain to them that they should press down onto the footrests using their calf and thigh muscles and to lean back slightly to compensate for the forces acting on the bike. Braking should be started earlier in order to compensate for the extra weight and cornering the bike might take extra input and impetus from you, the rider. The example on the left shows what happens during braking if the pillion isn't holding on. Having your pillion's body and helmet slamming in to you every time you break is something you'll quickly tire of. By leaning back during braking, as shown on the right, you'll be able to concentrate on the road fully.

Loading your bike with - for example - camping gear for a weekend will add extra weight so you will need to alter your tyre pressures and suspension settings to suit. Take care not to overload you bike, or exceed the capacity of any luggage rack / pannier bracket etc. Never carry anything on the bike which is wider than the handlebars. Also remember that it is against the law to carry an insecure, unstable or oversized load. Never attempt to ride your bike if it is over-loaded, and you'll know when you've overloaded it because the handlebars will turn from side to side. like a slow-speed tank-slapper, as you try to set-off.

Take extra care when accelerating with a load which is heavier than you are normally used to carrying on your bike. During hard acceleration with heavy luggage and a pillion, the front end of the bike might (most probably) seem to feel 'light,' as the effect of weight-transference shifts towards the rear of the bike. Care must be taken at that point so as not to cause the machine to 'wheelie' as hard acceleration with a lot of weight transference going rear-wards, is the ideal breeding ground for a wheelie. Unwanted wheelies can be eliminated by closing the throttle gently, changing up a gear or by applying gentle pressure to the back brake. Whichever method you use, expect a rough landing when the bike's front wheel lands again. As long as the bike is travelling in a straight line and is upright, you shouldn't have too many problems as the bike will right itself due to gyroscopic effects acting on the front wheel.

When carrying luggage and panniers, it might be easier for the pillion to get on to the riders seat first and then slide back into the pillion seat, then the rider can get on.

With a large-capacity bike, or a bike which is heavier due to a pillion and luggage there's a simple trick to use whilst you're cornering. Basically, you need to reduce the bike's Centre-of-Gravity (CoG) and that can be done easily by reducing the distance between your shoulders and your wrists. All you need to do is bend forward slightly and bend your elbows. Also, by inching your bum across the seat, in the same direction as the bend, as you enter the bend will also help lower your CoG, but, be warned, it's a skill which requires practice and fore-thought.

Braking will take more input from the rider and will take a greater distance if the bike is two-up and loaded as there will be a lot more weight-transference travelling forwards during braking. This can tire a rider out very quickly, particularly if travelling on roads which require a lot of braking / accelerating such as roads through hilly countryside or mountainous regions.

Likewise, cornering will take a greater effort as you will need to counter-act the effects of the Mass of the bike, rider, pillion and luggage against the gyroscopic effects acting upon the front wheel. It goes without saying that the faster you go, the more weight you are carrying, the more input onto the handlebars you'll have to exert.

'Biker's Code'

As bikers, we are a minority, so we should help each other out wherever possible. If you see a bike broken-down you should try to stop (**iiistds**) and help. Obviously, DO NOT stop on the hard-shoulder of a motorway. You might not know much about bikes, but put yourself in that position, wouldn't you like somebody to stop and try to help ?

Also, when you're out and about on your bike you might see another rider nodding or waving at you. It doesn't mean that they've mistaken you for somebody else, they're just letting-on to a fellow biker. This usually happens on quieter roads, rather than in the middle of a city centre during rush-hour.

Bike Clubs

Meeting-up with fellow bikers at a local 'biker haunt' is a great way to make friends with like-minded people. If you don't know any in the area, your local motorcycle mechanics or bike shop might be a good place to start.

Some motorcycle dealerships will encourage customers (and their friends) to come down on a Saturday morning to pull a few clutch levers, kick a few tyres, and generally make the place look busy. Some dealerships will arrange Track Days or Off-road days for a particular marque as a Factory-sponsored promotion.

If you're looking for a more active social life with fellow bikers, then perhaps you could try your local Motorcycle club. Bike clubs in the UK are split into two categories, either MCC or MC, and I'll describe the difference for you.

MCC - Motor Cycle Club -These are usually based around at a 'Biker-friendly' pub on a set time / night of the week. MCCs are usually created by a bunch of mates which want to form a 'collective'. MCCs are normally run as a Democracy, with Members voting on Club decisions, presided by the Chairman. The Membership process to join an MCC varies nearly as much as the types of MCC that there are, with some requiring nothing more than you turning-up 3 weeks in a row. Other, more established clubs, may have a more stringent process for Prospective members. Some MCCs will have a 'Club Patch' which can be worn anywhere EXCEPT on the back of the jacket / cut-off. To make it perfectly clear, MCC patches can ONLY be worn on the sleeves, front or sides of your jacket / cut-off. Here's a piece of advice on the subject, MC Clubs will not take very kindly to anybody imitating a character from an 'Outlaw Biker' film or TV series. I cannot stress this enough, DON'T !.

Rallys / Biker Parties

Organised by larger bike clubs or Organisations, these are week-end long events aimed specifically at bikers, by bikers, for bikers. Usually held in the more remote locations, it's a great way to spend the weekend - camping in a field with your mates (or on your own) - chilaxin'. As an analogy, I'd say they're a bit like a 'miniature Glastonbury', only a lot cheaper.

Camping on a motorbike

Whether it's an organised event, or you and a few mates decide on a road trip, you're going to need to carry a fair amount of kit. The trick is to pack as light as possible but there are limits. A mountaineer's tent will be tiny and light to pack, but when you put it up there'll be nowhere for your helmet etc to fit. My recommendation would be to add an extra person to your tent. In other words, if your going on your own, buy a 2-man tent but if you're going with your 'other half' (or whoever), then get a 3-man tent. The reason is simple, all of your bike kit takes-up the room of a person ! Air-beds are heavy and you'll need a pump to inflate it, whereas 'camping mats' are lighter, but nowhere near as comfy ! Sleeping bags are 'tog-rated' so choose one to suit your needs but it's probably a good idea to get a sleeping bag which goes below the temperatures you're expecting to be camping in. You never know ! Buy yourself a 'Sidestand Puck' as these great inventions help stop your bike's sidestand sinking into the grass. Drill a small hole through it near the edge, and attach some para-cord / guy-rope to it and loop the other end around your handlebar. When you want to set-off, you don't have to stoop down to pick it up.

Carrying luggage

There's 2 basic types of luggage - 'soft' or 'hard'. Soft luggage includes 'Throwover' panniers / saddle bags and are made from textile / leather soft PVC, whereas 'hard' luggage is usually made of aluminium, fibreglass or rigid plastic. Hard luggage also requires the bike to be fitted with a bracket system, to which the hard luggage attaches. If you're going to use soft luggage, check that the back of the panniers (for example) doesn't rub on the bike's paintwork. One solution is to place a soft towel over the seat so that it drapes down on both sides of the bike before you fit the panniers. Another solution is to put masking tape over your paintwork first.

If you're carrying a pillion and use soft luggage, chances are that you'll need a rack. Most racks come with a pillion 'grab-handle', or else they'll incorporate the bike's grab-handle.

A rack will give you an extra place upon which to secure your gear and there's plenty of places to fasten to. Most bikes don't usually have an abundance of safe hooking points. Use Bungee cords / straps, Bungee nets or nylon ratchet straps to fasten your gear securely to your bike. After all, you don't want to ride 50 miles (or whatever) to arrive at your destination and discover that your kit is at the side of the road somewhere near your home. (On top of that, it's 3 penalty points on your licence if your load is deemed to be insecure by the arresting Officer.) Once you've secured your luggage, give it a good shake and check that the bike moves as much as the luggage does.

Here's an example of 'hard' luggage. Notice that the 'grab-handles' for the pillion are at the sides which, in this example, are actually part of the support frame for the hard luggage.

The top-box will also help to stop a pillion from flying off the back during heavy acceleration.

Remember, don't pack anything heavy high-up as this will greatly affect the bike's handling.

Riding in a group – Riding in a group is something which you may end-up doing at some point and you'll need to know the safest method. Riding one bike behind the other doesn't give anybody, except the leading rider, a clear view ahead. If the leading bike brakes sharply, there will be insufficient time or space, three of four bikes back, to be able to stop and a collision will happen. The safest way is to form two lines so that each bike can still leave a safe gap between it and the bike in front. One column rides on the right-hand side of the lane and the other rides nearer to the centre white line. The outer column should then ride so that each bike is half-way between two of the bikes in the left-hand column. Riding in such a way will not only reduce the amount of overall

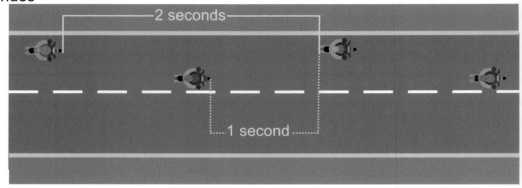

length of road taken-up but will also increase the all-round visibility for each of the riders. This method is ideal if you are riding in a convoy such as a charity run etc as it leaves room for the marshalls to overtake safely.

Always remember, especially when riding in a small group, that the 2 second rule is a **bare-minimum** rule of thumb and doesn't apply at higher speeds. If you need a reminder, just look back at the diagrams at the beginning of this chapter.

This diagram represents a small group of riders travelling in single file at 30 (or whatever) MPH .

This rider sees a hazard up-ahead and brakes hard.

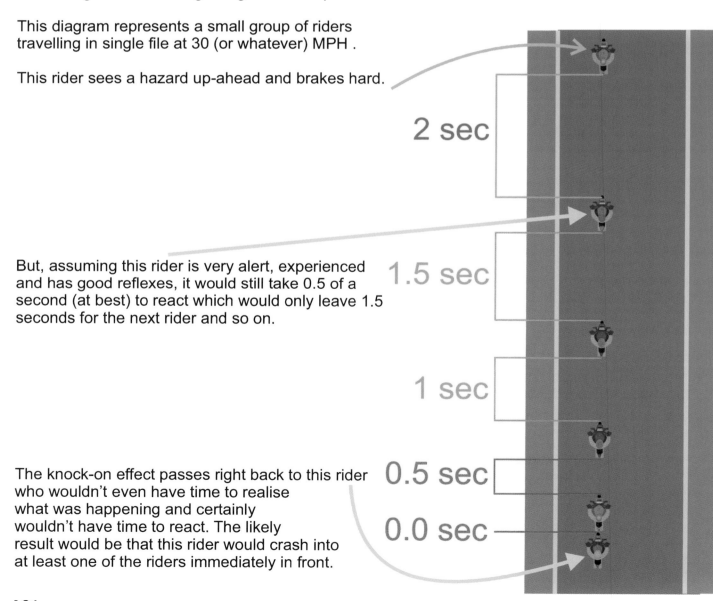

But, assuming this rider is very alert, experienced and has good reflexes, it would still take 0.5 of a second (at best) to react which would only leave 1.5 seconds for the next rider and so on.

The knock-on effect passes right back to this rider who wouldn't even have time to realise what was happening and certainly wouldn't have time to react. The likely result would be that this rider would crash into at least one of the riders immediately in front.

2 sec

1.5 sec

1 sec

0.5 sec

0.0 sec

Let's now look at wet roads and in particular, we'll look at the painted lines on the road's surface which can be across the width, along the middle or along the sides of the lane.

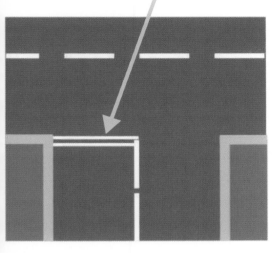
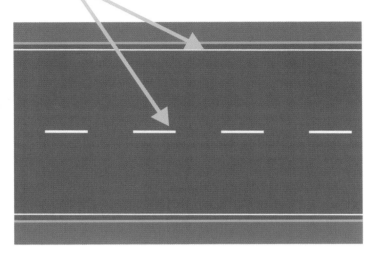

Tarmac is a fairly good material to give your tyres something to stick to but painted lines aren't made of tarmac ! The paint itself creates a lump on the road's surface which, particularly on a smaller machine with thinner tyres, can disrupt the bike's handling. Let's take a look at the actual shape of a road's surface seen as a cross-section :-

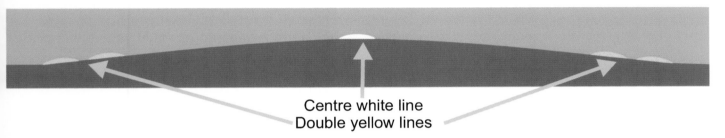

Centre white line
Double yellow lines

You can clearly see how the raised area of the road's surface could cause your bike to wobble or weave, especially at low speeds. How much impact the painted line has on your bike's stability also depends on the condition and age of the painted line. Whereas a newly painted line might be quite smooth and even, an old, neglected one might be breaking-up in places, leaving an uneven road surface for you to ride on.

You will probably have to ride over the centre white line frequently if you need to overtake other vehicles which are parked-up, or other road users who are moving, so include scanning the road's surface ahead of you as part of your constant Forward Hazard Assessment. In wet conditions, it might sometimes feel as if your tyres lose grip temporarily as you cross the centre white line but don't worry about it, it's perfectly normal and over in a millisecond or two ... Also, despite what you might think, the bike hardly moves !

Many towns and cities will, invariably, have extremely busy junctions similar to the one shown on the right and as a general rule "the more paint, the more restraint" You're better off adjusting your speed accordingly on your approach to such a junction.

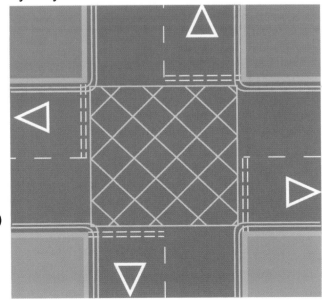

The rule for box junctions is very easy :- DO NOT enter unless your exit is clear, EXCEPT when you're turning right (or queueing behind other traffic to do so) and the only thing stopping you is on-coming traffic. (Highway Code Rule #174)

Another type of painted line to keep an eye out for is the one designed to make all road-users "aware of their speed" and can often be found at exit slip-roads and roundabouts on dual-carriageways, and look something like this :-

The intention of these lines is to "bring to your attention that there is a need for you reduce your speed" but, on a motorbike, these things can sometimes feel like mini speed-ramps - meaning that your bike's suspension will be working overtime ! You will need to give yourself an extra little bit of braking distance (especially in the wet) to allow for the fact that you can't break as hard as you would be able to if the lines weren't there. (Which might seem a bit strange, once you've thought about their original purpose ...)

Rainbows in the road ? Unless you're on mind-altering drugs, this should warn you that there is oil, petrol or diesel on the road. It won't be as clear as this picture shows, so I've included a 'real-world' photo for comparison :-

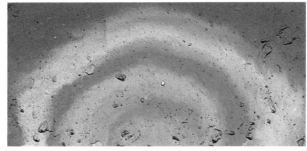

This effect can be caused by only a few drops of oil, petrol or diesel reacting to a damp road surface and can prove to be a very tricky riding surface. It's also the favourite excuse for a lot of bad riders who throw their bikes into the ditches when cornering ! Everybody knows that oil and water don't mix but when you throw a rubber tyre into the equation, things can get very slippery indeed. A small (fist-sized) patch of diesel spill shouldn't give you too much cause for concern but a larger patch might be quite a problem, especially if you're banked-over. Don't overly-worry yourself though if you see that you're about to ride right over a 6 inch patch of oil, and certainly don't panic and do an Emergency Stop. Think about it for a second .... If you travel 44ft in one second, then you travel 6 inches in 0.068 seconds. Oh, and if you've got really good reflexes, it'll take you about 0.5 seconds to react anyway. Just try to avoid the obvious larger patches when you can **(iiistds),** watch your speed and give yourself plenty of room between you and the vehicle you're following, if possible, to see more of the road ahead. Fuel / oil patches are very common on roundabouts due to vehicles 'overfilling' their fuel tanks.

Engine oil, gearbox oil, petrol, diesel and the rubber for your tyres are all manufactured from the same base ingredient, crude oil, but imagine what happens when your oil-covered tyre meets a wet surface.

After riding at high speed for a while you will become accustomed so care must be exercised when entering a lower speed limit zone as everything will artificially seem slow to you. Traffic, including yourself, will appear to be crawling along so it's a good idea to keep an eye on your bike's speedo until you fully readjust and re-acclimatise to the speed and traffic conditions which can take up to about 10 minutes.

When approaching a left-hand side-road, be prepared for vehicles exiting from it and turning left whilst casually glancing to their right. In that situation, immediately consider using the horn as well as the brakes. Your road position would normally be over towards the centre white line in that situation as that would give you the best reaction time. If, as you approach the same junction, the car is stationary, then don't bother looking at the driver. Instead, watch the front, offside wheel and tyre for any movement <u>whatsoever</u> as that will tell you the millisecond the vehicle moves. As before, immediately consider using the horn as well as the brakes. The same rule can be applied if a vehicle is turning right or going straight-across from a right-hand junction and has stopped at the centre white line, watch for wheel or tyre movement. Again, immediately consider using the horn as well as the brakes.

Riding at night is totally different that riding in daylight but the rules of BikerCraft's System still apply. In certain circumstances, it is easier to spot a potential hazard, or to use another vehicle as a

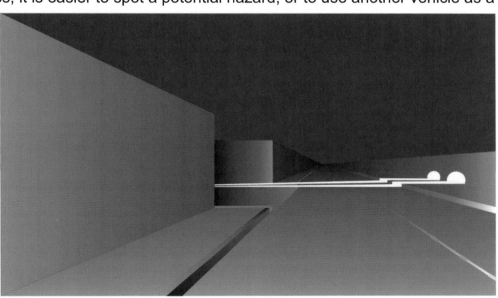

forewarning as to what the road is like further up ahead. In this example, a vehicle is approaching the junction on an un-lit road from your left. You can't see the car, but you can see that it's projecting it's headlights onto the walls to your right. You'd be able to recognise that a car could be approaching the Give Way lines. The car might stop, it might slow-down or it might just pull out ... In this case, Lifesaver (right) and pull-out more towards the centre white line.

In this picture, you're on an unfamiliar, unlit road in the middle of nowhere. By keeping an eye on the tail-lights lights of the car in front of you, you can have an idea of the layout of the road. If that car's brake-lights come on, you can expect a severe bend, maybe a junction or another potential hazard lies up-ahead. That information could help you to make an early assessment of the road and what actions you might need to take. Another handy tip is how to deal with the on-coming

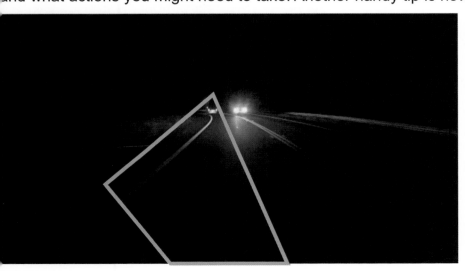

car's headlights. In order to avoid being dazzled by on-coming traffic's headlights or main-beam by averting your eyes to the kerb, or side of the road, well ahead of you to your left. Doing this will still allow for you to see the direction of the road etc, but your night-vision will not be ruined. This technique takes time to master as you will feel drawn, for some reason, to look directly at the car's headlights ....

Keeping an eye out on a vehicle's brake lights in front of you will give you an indication that you may need to slow down further along. If there's a vehicle following you which may be too close for comfort, one way of making the other road user aware of their proximity is to lightly apply your rear brake pedal, just enough to activate the brake switch but not the brakes. This technique should cause the other road user to slow down which might help to put some distance between you and the following vehicle. If the vehicle remains at a close position it might be better to let the other vehicle pass, when safe to do so. If the following vehicle has left it's main beam on, a couple of light taps on the rear brake pedal, as before, might help them to realise that they have left their main beam on. Do not try to look at the vehicle in your mirrors as you might end-up being night-blinded, putting you in a very serious predicament.

If you're executing a Lifesaver, ensure that your rearward vision is not impeded or affected by the glare of the headlights. Do not use sunglasses, tinted visors or the helmet's sun-visor at night, because whilst it may reduce the glare from other road user's headlights, it will seriously impede your ability to spot anything which is unlit that would normally be visible, as these graphics show:-

Unlit road with clear visor.

The same shot, except, as seen through a dark visor.

On unlit roads, the use of the motorcycle's main beam will allow a better view of the road ahead but care must be taken so as to not dazzle on-coming traffic or other road users that you are following. Dipping the main beam whilst going over hump-backed bridges or when negotiating a left-hand bend or turn will help keep the road illuminated for you. If a visual warning signal is required at night, pressing the 'pass' button, usually on the left-hand side of your handlebars, will give you the maximum amount of light possible as it will keep the headlight on normal beam whilst activating the main beam at the same time. Flashing your headlight once should alert any other road user that they have left their main beam on. Never retaliate by switching your main beam on as that could dazzle the other road user and possibly cause an accident. When entering an unlit stretch of road from a lit stretch, allow time for your eyes to become accustomed to the lack of light. Humans have evolved into day-light living creatures whose eyes require time to readjust to the dark.

Another thing to bear in mind is that there is a period during dawn and dusk when the light is such that everything unlit will appear to lose it's colour and appear as black, white or a shade of grey and extreme care must be taken when riding in those conditions. During dark periods, distances will seem different than during daylight hours, which must be allowed for if you are always going to be able to stop within the visible distance that you have. Use whatever information you can to try and glean an advantage as to what road conditions may lie ahead. Watch for another road user's lights coming towards you as they approach a bend. The car's lights either will sweep gently around the bend or show, by a quicker sweep, that the bend could be severe.

Riding in strong side-winds can be a harrowing experience, even for experienced riders, especially if it's a sudden, unexpected gust when riding on wet roads. Keep calm, try not to tense-up, and gently lean your upper body into the wind whilst keeping the bike upright and going in the right direction.

Motorways / Dual Carriageways

Generally speaking, dual-carriageways and motorways form the artery of the country's transportation network and as such, carry enormous volumes of traffic. Speeds on these types of roads are normally much higher than in built-up areas but can vary massively from one lane to another.

The National speed limit in the UK is 70 MPH but always be prepared for other vehicles travelling at much higher speeds. Speeding is one of the most commonly broken laws but, unfortunately, so is poor lane discipline. Most drivers seem unaware to the fact that you should always be in the left-most lane (otherwise referred to as lane 1) **unless** you are overtaking another vehicle. Road-users who unnecessarily 'hog' the middle lane (lane 2) effectively turn a three-lane road into a two-lane road due to the fact that it is illegal to pass another vehicle on the inside.

Vehicles pulling onto a motorway or dual-carriageway from the slip-road can easily create of knock-on effect of vehicles pulling out from the left-most lane as they allow other traffic to join the motorway. Use the road signs to give yourself advance warning as to this potential hazard, take rear-observations to assess the traffic which is not only directly behind you, but also in the lane(s) behind you, to your right. As soon as you can see the traffic travelling along the slip-road, assess the speed of those vehicles and compare them to the speed of the vehicles already travelling in the lane 1. If it obvious that you will need to move over to the next lane to your right, you can pro-actively take another rear-oservation, indicate, do a Lifesaver and move out to the next lane (iiistds) - all in plenty of time. (The green dotted line represents a potential 'escape route) In a situation like that, as you near the end of the slip-road, always be prepared for other road-users to suddenly indicate, pull-out whilst casually checking the door mirror - usually all done in one movement - right in front of you. If, in this particular scenario, you were already in the middle lane of a motorway, then be prepared for traffic moving from lane 1 into lane 2, which could cause some drivers to need to then pull-out into the outside lane. Also keep a vigilant watch-out for brain-dead, selfish drivers who think that they own the outside lane and feel that they must get from the slip-road and into the outside lane as quickly as possible.

Motorways and dual-carriageways usually offer greater forward vision than urban roads so you should always be looking well ahead - not just at the rear of the vehicle immediately in front of you but look over it, past it, through it. If you see a large lorry pull into lane 2 ahead, then you will know that the speed in lane 2 will be no more than 58 MPH as that is the maximum speed allowed for HGVs. The current European limit is 56 MPH, but some companies chose to restrict down to 48 MPH to conserve fuel. By looking well ahead, you will be able to give yourself more reaction time to avoid such hazards. Constantly watch, assess and compare the course and speeds of vehicles in the other lane(s) next to the lane you are using. If, for example, you are using lane 2 and notice up ahead that a faster-moving car in lane 1 is approaching a slower-moving lorry, then you can start to think about manoeuvering into lane 3. Watch for other vehicles drifting towards the lane you are using by keeping an eye on the distance between the tyres and the white lines. If this distance is tapering, then you have 3 choices :-

1) Accelerate (iiistds)   2) Brake (iiistds)   3) Pull into the next lane if possible (iiistds)

If you're going to accelerate, remember what happens when you double your speed ! If, as you accelerate, the vehicle in front of you brakes, then you are creating more problems for yourself. If you choose to brake, then traffic behind you might not have the Reaction Time or Braking Distance to avoid running into the back of you. Pulling out, into the next lane to your right, would be a more practical, sensible manoeuvre, but only if you've been paying attention, only if you've been observing properly and know what's going-on all around you. Concentration / Observation at all times ...

When going from an urban environment onto a motorway, you might need to allow yourself a little time in order for your brain to acclimatise to the higher speeds. Make sure that you have enough fuel to complete your journey or reach the Services and remember that it is illegal to stop on a motorway except in the event of an emergency, so if the weather looks like it might rain, dress accordingly.

If you are approaching an exit slip-road on a motorway, whether you're in lane 1 or 2, take a Lifesaver over your right shoulder to spot if any other vehicles are going to suddenly swerve in order to make the exit. You can help yourself by keeping a near-constant eye on your mirrors when approaching a slip-road.

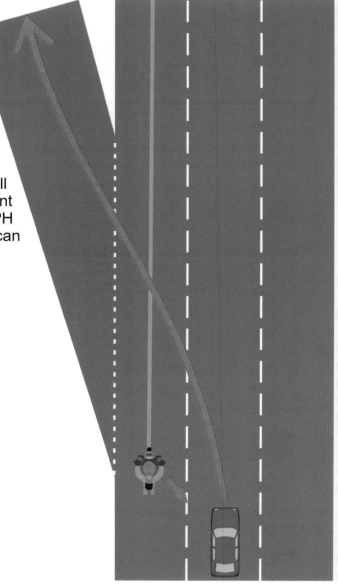

Everything will seem strangely slow as your brain will still be thinking at motorway speeds so keep a vigilant eye on your speedo. 30 MPH will not feel like 30 MPH until your brain readapts to the environment, which can take up to about 10 minutes.

Communication

Bluetooth helmet sets, bike-to-bike and rider-to-pillion intercom systems are common-place gadgets but their use must be given serious consideration as they are all a totally un-necessary distraction. Riding a motorbike requires an **enormous** amount of constant **Concentration,** constant **Forward Hazard-Assessment,** constant decision-making and the question you've got to ask yourself is this "could I do all of the above whilst having a casual conversation ?" If your brain is concentrating on having a conversation, it will have to stop concentrating on everything else going-on around you because nobody's brain can process two things simultaneously. GPS systems are a fantastic aid to navigation but care must be given to ensure that none of your manoeuvres are rushed, or omitted altogether, in order to follow the sat-nav's commands. A hastily executed turn will put you, and those around you, at serious risk of harm or injury. It's a Sat-nav, so it'll get you there even if you miss *that* particular junction. Allow for other road-users to commit the same fault.

How much time would this biker spend actually concentrating on the road ?

Parking-up

I suppose Rule Number One on this subject is to always leave your bike parked in first gear if you're using the side-stand. In doing so, it's less likely to roll off it's side-stand and break or scrape something expensive. If you're parking at the side of the road, remember that roads have cambers sloping down towards the gutter. I would suggest always parking your bike with the rear tyre touching the kerb. There are two reasons for this piece of advice :-

1)   If the bike's in gear, it shouldn't move at all.
2)   It will be easier for you to ride away from the kerb, rather than have to drag your bike backwards, up the camber, out into the road.

Don't forget to secure your bike.

Dropped your bike ?

The trick is to get your handlebars on full lock and then turn your back to the machine so that you can use your thigh muscles, and not your back muscles, when you come to lift the bike. If the bike's lying on it's right, you would grab the handlebar on the throttle side with your left hand and if your bike's lying on it's left-hand side, you would use the handlebar at the clutch lever side with your right hand. With you back against the saddle, grip the handlebar with the relevant hand and then find a suitable place to grip your machine with your other hand whilst your legs are slightly bent. Then, use your leg muscles to power your legs straight and lift the bike up. Use your thighs to steady the bike until it is back upright and you can then lower the side-stand. There's a video that you can watch at https://www.youtube.com/watch?v=cWrsyP1tJuM which makes the method perfectly clear and saves me writing any more !!

You'll probably need to reset your mirror(s) if they're not smashed and you'll also need to check that your handlebar levers are operable and that the throttle, back brake pedal or gear change (depending on which side you dropped it) work and double-check that your indicators are still attached and working. Look closely at the road where the motorcycle fell / crashed to see if there are any broken bits lying around. At the same time, look for signs of any fluid which may have leaked out.

Concentration / Observation

This is the one thing that I've been trying to drum into you throughout the entire book and there's a reason for that. If you don't do both of these, at all times when riding, then you're just an accident looking for somewhere to happen ! Whenever you start to put your bike gear on, as you fire your bike up, remember :- **Riding Rule #1**. Switch your brain into 'Riding Mode' and keep it like that until your journey's finished. Don't just 'look' at the road ahead, <u>scan</u> it ! Keep moving your eyes all around your field of vision, constantly, and get used to using your peripheral vision to help as well. By moving your eyes around, small, minute changes will be detected by your brain. If a car or pedestrian moves, you'll spot it !

Lifesavers

As you learn to adopt BikerCraft into your everyday riding, Lifesavers should become fully automatic. If you think about it, they're just an addition to Concentration / Observation because you're observing behind you. Let's bring back a couple of pictures from Chapter 1 :-

Have a guess what would happen if the rider in this picture turned or pulled-out to the right ?

All it takes is a Lifesaver ...!

It's irrelevant how many years you've been riding for. It's irrelevant how many miles you've ridden or how good you think that you and / or the bike is. Idiots happen everywhere and whenever you're on a bike, it's up to you to spot them before they do you any damage.

Also, as you get to be a better and more confident rider, you might decide to get a faster bike and here's another perfectly good reason why you should always keep an eye on what's behind you by doing regular Lifesavers. Remember, your mirrors are pretty useless and have massive blind-spots.

This rider might've been on a good Course / Line exiting some nice bends and see a long, straight, clear road ahead. The biker might even be speeding a (little) bit - but was checking the mirrors at exactly the same time as this photo was taken ...

... but look what the rider would have seen, had a Lifesaver been done ! Whatever your first reaction is, the next question in your head will be "how long's that bike been there for ?" Depends on when you stopped **Concentrating / Observing**, I suppose !

Loud exhausts

There's an old saying "loud pipes save lives"which refers to fitting after-market, non-standard exhausts to the bike. There's 2 sides to this argument. Yes, you will be heard by all and sundry every time you take you bike out, but you might have to take your neighbours into consideration if you work early or late shifts. The downside is that the same bellowing exhaust will also be heard by Traffic Officers, giving them advance warning of your approach !

Also, if you're accelerating hard and hit (a false) neutral in your bike's gearbox, everybody's going to hear your bike's engine screaming before it either hits the rev-limiter or self-destructs !

In heavily pedestrianised areas, don't assume that everybody will be aware of you because of your bike's loud exhaust. Podestrians etc might not have a clue that you're there so always be ready to sound the bike's horn as an advance warning of your presence.

Travelling by ferry

There may come a time, for whatever reason, that you need to cross on a ferry so it's important for you to know how to secure your bike, because it's your responsibility. Where bikes are parked, there are lengths of rope provided for you to tie your bike down to the metal loops in the ship's deck. Use your centre-stand (if fitted) or else park the bike in 1st gear on the side-stand and place the rope loosely over your seat. Next, secure the rope onto the metal loop on the right-hand side (as you sit on it) of the bike and then place your gloves between the rope and your bike's seat before you feed the rope through the metal loop on the left-hand side of the bike. If possible, have somebody apply some body-weight to the bike in order to compress the suspension slightly, use the metal loop as a pulley to tension the rope and tie it off. The reason for placing your gloves on the seat is so that the rope won't cause an expensive rip or tear to your seat cover, and anybody who's sat on a torn seat cover will testify that it takes weeks to dry out after it's rained ! And by the way, gaffer tape never works for very long ....

Riding abroad

In all but a few countries, riding abroad means riding on the opposite side of the road but BikerCraft's System still applies by switching left for right and right for left. In mainland Europe, for example, instead of junctions to your left being the most hazardous, it will be junctions on the right. A right turn will be as straight-forward as a left turn is in the UK but a left turn will be similar to a right turn. Rear observations would be over your left shoulder and at roundabouts you give way to traffic coming from your left. Traffic signs are usually self-explanatory wherever you go but it might be an idea to jump on the 'net and do some research before you go.

When you're riding abroad, take your time to fully familiarise yourself with the roads and traffic and sometimes it's a good idea to follow a local, native, vehicle until you feel that your are accustomed. Generally speaking and based purely on personal experience, the standard of car driving is much higher in countries like Holland, Germany and Belgium but the same can't be said for places like Asia and the Far East.

Final thoughts

Riding a motorcycle, despite our modern, congested, over-crowded roads, can still give you a sense of freedom, thrill and excitement. It can be the most fun that you can have with your clothes on ! Gaining confidence, knowledge and experience will only enhance your enjoyment of riding your motorcycle but as your skills, knowledge and experience increase, you must NEVER allow yourself to become over-confident. Every mile you spend riding, learning and practising BikerCraft's System will help you to add to your arsenal of knowledge for the future. When you stop needing to memorise or recite BikerCraft's System, when you stop needing to think about changing gear or being in the best possible position at all times, then you will be well on the way to mastering the skills necessary. Through proper riding and constant application of BikerCraft's System you will become a more confident, capable and safer rider who will enjoy the art of motorcycling even more. If we go back to the music analogy at the very beginning of this book, you're now a musical maestro who makes playing complicated tunes on any instrument look easy.

It is a true fact that you never stop learning to ride a motorbike until the day that you die. Hopefully, that day will be a long way off but in the meantime, enjoy it to the full and remember to make the most of it.

Take care, have fun, ride safe.

Printed in Great Britain
by Amazon